Reaching for Higher Thought

Reading Writing Thinking Strategies

Faye Brownlie   Susan Close   Linda Wingren

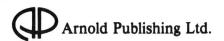Arnold Publishing Ltd.

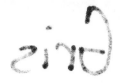

Arnold Publishing Ltd.
10301 - 104 Street
Edmonton, Alberta, Canada T5J 1B9
Phone: (403) 426-2998
Fax: (403) 426-4607

Authors: Faye Brownlie
Susan Close
Linda Wingren

Edited by Nancy Marcotte

Designed and Typeset by Andrea Carter

Cover Design by Kim Young

Photographs by Daphne Clifton and Bob York

Assistance with Student Lettering by Chenoa Marcotte

ISBN 0-919913-42-3

PRINTED IN CANADA
by The Jasper Printing Group
Edmonton, Alberta

Dedicated to all of the children who have helped us learn

Acknowledgements

Many, many people have helped us make this book a reality. To them all we extend hearty "thanks" for their skill, their coaching, and especially their patience.

Thanks to the organizers of the Richmond Young Writers' Institute 1981 for bringing us together and stimulating our thinking.

Thanks to students and teachers for the opportunities to learn in:

Chilliwack School District 33, British Columbia
Langley School District 35, British Columbia
Richmond School District 38, British Columbia
Lord Selkirk School District 11, Manitoba

Thanks to Daphne Clifton and Bob York for their photographs.
Thanks to Kim Young for the cover design.
Thanks for countless hours of after-hour typing to secretaries Maureen Crerar, Sandi Prunkle, and Sandy Whitehurst.

We appreciate the work of Gabriele Lusser Rico and her search for strategies to realize the potential in all students. Her unfailing belief in the power of all minds gave us the confidence and inspiration to explore connections and to create new strategies.

Contents

The authors reflect on their arrival at a series of strategies that are teacher-directed, student-centred, and skill-built. These collaborative strategies enhance student learning as they guide students toward becoming independent, thoughtful learners.

The theoretical background is presented. An integrated approach blending the reading, writing, speaking, and listening processes results in a new reading/writing cycle. All strategies flow from speaking and listening to reading and writing.

The foundation of powerful writing is ably using what you know in a creative, productive fashion. The use of imagery and clustering prior to drafting heightens the power of the writing.

The interrelationship of the reading/writing process is explored as students share their thinking, cluster their thoughts during an oral reading of text, and write in role.

Building from prior knowledge in an oral language classroom, students' conceptual knowledge is developed by collecting group information and categorizing this, as a class, prior to a unit of study.

Prior to reading a text, students in small groups categorize vocabulary words and predict what questions will be answered in the text.

Students bring to reading a strong sense of story. Using this schema as a base, the class predicts, then reads to confirm, the elements of story found in a piece of text.

Introduction

Reaching For Higher Thought is not only predicated on the idea
of the *active* learner, it also demonstrates how we can achieve
such learner involvement through strategies that elicit both new
and renewed commitments to teaching.

In ***Reaching For Higher Thought*** the written product and the
reading of a text are only the tip of the iceberg of a series of thinking and doing strategies designed to involve learners profoundly in
the thinking/learning experience. The book provides a fresh and
important pedagogical angle precisely because it focuses on the
normally silent and invisible—and primarily untapped—thinking
processes represented by the iceberg below the water.

Reaching For Higher Thought does not merely talk about thinking—it illustrates thinking; it is a book about integrating listening,
writing, and reading through such prewriting/reading strategies as
imagining, clustering, questioning, anticipating; it is a book about
enabling learners to explore their own thinking processes; it is a
book about collaborative learning; it is a book about honing what
readers already know. It is a book about learning as involvement at
emotional, cognitive, and metacognitive levels, focusing on bringing the rest of the iceberg to light by generating activities that encourage learners to wonder, predict, remember, support, connect,
guess, and play; most of all it is a book about unlearning our tradi-
tional teaching roles as authorities and relearning more effective
roles as facilitators and elicitors of strategies and skills that lead the
learner to thinking and genuine feelings of success.

In ***Reaching For Higher Thought*** learners perceive themselves as
"readers" as well as "writers", as sharers as well as listeners, as
tellers as well as questioners, as fact-finders as well as wonderers,

as editors as well as proud publishers. Throughout these stages, neither the tip of the iceberg nor the infinitely larger, invisible ''thinking'' mass is ignored but is perceived as connected and brought into the learner's awareness.

Best of all, the higher thinking strategies illustrated here simplify rather than complicate our enormous tasks as teachers, leading us to the profound pleasure accompanying our recognition that students are willing, active, and successful participants in their own learning experience.

In sum, this book is a thought-quest that focuses on wholeness, on organic approaches to learning, and on learner empowerment.

Gabriele Rico
Cambridge, Massachusetts
June 6, 1988
author of *Writing the Natural Way*

Journey to Connections

Linda Wingren   Susan Close

The challenge of presenting our collaborative thinking has charged our lives with energy. The discipline and rigour involved in getting inside our experiences has led us to insights that might not have been otherwise possible. Many, many teachers in workshops have pressed us to share our understandings. In this book we present our current thinking about a teacher-directed, student-centred, skill-built approach to learning.

All three of us have had the opportunity to step briefly away from daily classroom life, to reflect, and to design. We have approached the helping role by listening to questions, bouncing ideas off colleagues, combing research, planning learning sequences, observing students as they reach for language that matches their thinking, listening to students reflect on how they learn, then modifying and expanding our repertoire to generate anew.

Faye Brownlie

Reverberating through all of what we do is the utmost respect for teachers and learners. We know there is no single, exclusive "right" way. Teaching will always be a balance of art and science. What is new for us is the development of a beginning set of strategies. These strategies pull together what research is showing about conditions under which people learn best and how neurologists believe the brain processes information. As we have field-tested each strategy, we have been truly humbled by how each allows student minds to open to expanding cycles of thinking and leads students to advancing levels of language complexity. The universal application has a calming effect. In a time when curricular demands grow, we find comfort in being able to draw upon strategies that will lessen preparation and marking time while enhancing student learning time.

Reaching For Higher Thought is an exciting synthesis of the experiences of three minds, strengthened by connections with thousands of teachers and many more students—in all grades and in curricula representing all ability levels. It is an early contribution to an emerging body of knowledge. It is also our attempt to clarify what makes a difference, what we actually do with students, and what these vibrant learning environments look like and sustain for learners.

Our intent is to develop the big picture as we work alongside you in a workshop setting. With trained eyes you will observe the teacher and students flow through each of the strategies. You will also hear the teacher reflect on what she is doing while she is doing it. At the end of each demonstration, the teacher will share further dimensions of the strategy, show samples of student work, and leave you with a thumbnail sketch of the strategy that could be used in a day book. In the final chapter we will hear from teachers in the field. They will share reflections on their implementation of the strategies and learning processes.

We invite you into our classrooms of the late 1980s. Join in our discussions. Take part in the challenges of the possibilities inherent in this approach to creating insightful learners. We aim to create thoughtful learners, sharing with them the results of our ongoing search for the best and our blend of research and experience. Language and thinking are the tools students use while acquiring, using, and creating knowledge within content areas. Our goal is to help students gain independence in learning so they will increase their control over the limitless possibilities of their minds. Gaining a working mastery of our strategies will allow you the teacher, like an orchestra leader, a commanding role in generating a vital sound—enthusiastic young voices expressing active learning. Students will use their language in the growing complexity of its potential to express the new and unique connections their minds make. We expect you will find, as we are finding, the importance of whole-group instruction, small-group engagement, individual commitment, and practice as the context for the networking of thought. The collaborative strategies provide a social situation in which learning is both enjoyable and effective.

Our challenge to you is to participate with us, try out some of the ideas, listen to your children, share your thinking with a colleague, and develop new strategies to share. Growing together enriches us all.

Chapter

1

The Workshop

Each of the strategies in Chapters 2 to 12 is presented in a similar format. The **Classroom Story** runs the movie of the lesson, a movie depicting teachers and students learning together. In the classroom sits an observer, a novice to the strategy who comments on the lesson as it unfolds. **Teacher Thoughts** provide the commentary of the reflective practitioner, the teacher who critically examines the how and why of her actions and her language. We invite you into our classrooms as participants in our movies.

Great Great Grandmother

My great grandmother was an old lady. She died on February, the thirteenth, 1985 at 9:00. For a long time she lay lonely in a hospital bed. Visitors would come and go. People would have pity on her, for her suffering and loneliness. That can drown out someone's will to live. On Friday she let go of life. Now she lies silent, pleasant, without a fear, lost in her dreams.

That very night I had dreams of my own. This is how it went. Oh, gosh, where am I? Hey, I look like I'm in my grandma's place. I feel the striking pains in my stomach. I feel uncomfortable in my hospital bed. Days pass and sorrow grows over me. Then it ended. I was in a large box. I was put underground. I seemed to float through the box, extending underground, seeping to the roots of large trees, floating out of them, drifting higher through the clouds.

Suddenly I seemed to have appeared on the earth except, except that's it! This is a...a perfect world, no crime, violence, murder, no money, which leads to greed, no pollution, no wars, no smoking, no diseases, no death...

Scott, Grade 6

Scott wrote this draft in the spring of his first year in a writing process classroom. The class had sustained a passionate involvement with the novel *Where the Red Fern Grows*. The teacher had read from it often and at many different times of day, frequently leaving the children with author Wilson Rawls's words as they left school. She might start again at nine the next morning, sometimes responding to pleas from her Grade 6 class, other times just continuing with her planned goal of sustaining a literary environment for her students, keeping interest high by reading often and with all the drama the words demanded. Her enjoyment of literature and the value of sharing reading was apparent to her class. Scott and the rest were strongly caught up in the author's reality. They hunted and ran with the hounds. They cried softly behind their hands as Old Dan and Little Ann, the dogs, fought a mountain lion and died, one of fight wounds and the other of a broken heart. The language of the author went in incidentally. And it came out. Scott used the phrase, ''That can drown out someone's will to live.'' This, as well as his final line, ''a perfect world...,'' were borrowed from Rawls.

Poem Inspired by Wilson Rawls

The yellow arm reaching out
Clawing razor sharp
Scratches, deep and long
Taking a tight grip on the throat
The blood flows
Leaving a raging river.
It gurgles along the white oak leaves
The axe swings again and again
Blood stains on mangy fur
Fangs bared
They slowly sink in the red coat

It strikes again
Again they fight
Fatal this time
But no, he rears up
wanting to fight
wanting to be king
but that's not the way it is
when you fight the two hounds
and master—
nobody wins.
    Sheri, Grade 6

Sheri's poem was dedicated to Mr. Rawls. Mrs. Brown, the mother who helped by doing calligraphy for school poetry displays, said the vividness of the piece made her sick. She asked for less real writing please the next time she came.

See The Springtime
The songbirds sing notes on branches in the trees,
  sending a tune flowing through the breeze.
    They tell the world spring is here,
  Or spring is almost over, and summer is near.
  A chipmunk chatters a word to his tree,
    hoping it will also see.
    See, the crystal clear lake,
  as the water swirls like a spiraled snake.
   Enjoy the world, see it while you can,
  before it's over, your limited life span.
    Stephanie, Grade 6

Stephanie came to the process classroom already a very able writer. Her serious nature expressed itself in numerous poems of personal vision, which combined a sensitive seeing of nature with her gentle wisdom. She adorned the edges of her poetry pages with intricate illustrations, usually coloured in soft tones. She seemed to breathe in the patterns of authors whose writing she heard read aloud.

Herbie
Herbie, he lies in his crib, a sweet child no movement.
His little bright eyes tell me some of my future.
His hands attached to his stiff arms are lifeless as if venom had struck.
They move once in a while to figure his placing in life.
These hands of his are going to have a big part of his life.
Maybe a gymnast with golden medals.
His feet are squiggling and wiggling about.
Not knowing where he is or what he has to accomplish.
Herbie, this is only your beginning.
    Manpreet, Grade 6

Manpreet was a bold presenter. He looked forward to the power he felt when he stood behind a podium. It was his third year in a process classroom when he tossed off this draft, which he dedicated to his five-day-old brother, Herbie. The fact that there were ten or so teachers observing the fifty children combined from two classrooms, making an audience of sixty, delighted him all the more. His voice cut through awed and solemn silence. When he finished with "Herbie, this is only your beginning," he flashed a wide smile to his listeners. The observing teachers in the group later commented on the confidence of Manpreet and the students who presented with him. Theirs was a heady freedom as adults listened intently, responded genuinely to their writing, and asked them questions about their participation in the process classroom. The features of Frank Smith's literacy club, whose only admission requirement is that the members use written language, could hardly have been more perfectly demonstrated than by these fluent young writers who spoke of their craft and their experiences in learning to write. They didn't forget to mention what they had learned from authors whose stories they had loved hearing and reading themselves.

> There I stand like a baited bull
> at bay
> Stubborn and stupid
> I have the power of a Taurus
> and I'm ready to show them
> Face to face with reality
> What will I do but lower my head
> and charge
> twist and buck
> Throw off my pride
> Make a fool of myself
> But when the years wear on
> And I'm too weak to laugh
> Full heartedly
> I'll look back on these days
> And chuckle.
>
> Jeanie, Grade 4

Jeanie moved through her early months in a Grade 4 class anxious about writing especially, it seemed, since her classmates were more adept than she. However, the language of stories and her interest in animals, especially horses, combined in early drafts. She quickly came to understand that it was the effort that was acknowledged and responses were overwhelmingly positive. Her "pink pony in cave" stories were typical and she later said, though she tried hard to imagine, she couldn't do it at first. In Grades 5 and 6 her writing became an art. Jeanie would say her mother had to forbid her to read late into the night. Her large vocabulary and mastery of both poetry and prose were evident to everyone who heard or read her words. Imaging, she said, had become clear video-like movement. This is reminiscent of Enid Blyton's words.

"I shut my eyes for a few minutes with my portable typewriter on my knee. I make my mind a blank and wait and then, as clearly as I would see real children, my characters stand before me in my mind's eye."

Stone, 1974; as quoted by Michael T. Bagley in
Using Imagery in Creative Problem Solving

Jeanie said that while sometimes ideas came during an imagining beginning to a lesson or from a cluster, often she came to school knowing what she would write about that day. But it hadn't always been that easy to get started.

The place of literature was central to the development of all these students as readers and as writers. This was never more apparent than when they would occasionally sit through recess and lunch buzzers to hear more of a story that reached into their hearts and their minds.

When we reflect back on our early writing process classrooms, we can more clearly articulate the stages of the writing process. We can see our beginning recognition of the parallel processes of reading and writing. As we have learned from people like George Hillocks in the ERIC publication *Research on Written Composition*, we need to teach students how to become active learners.

We have field-tested these strategies with over ten thousand students in Kindergarten to Grade 10. They are a beginning, and they will develop. New strategies will emerge as we reach to learn with our students. As we ask new questions, research will help us with the answers. Echoing in our thoughts will always be Donald Graves's caution to avoid the creation of orthodoxies (unquestioned beliefs) or the lamination (locking into changelessness) of the process.

The Writing Process

Pre-Writing
—strategies to develop thinking

Drafting
—expressing thinking on paper
—reaching for language that matches thinking

Editing
—strategies for reworking text

Proofreading
—polishing the mechanics of writing

Publishing
—strategies to show the best draft

Presenting
—strategies to present pieces of writing to an audience

We have designed a **Writer's Cycle** as a framework that can be used in flexible ways depending on the teacher's purpose. Sometimes students will be writing to learn, other times they will be learning the craft of the writer, and at still other times they will be writing to read.

The Writer's Cycle

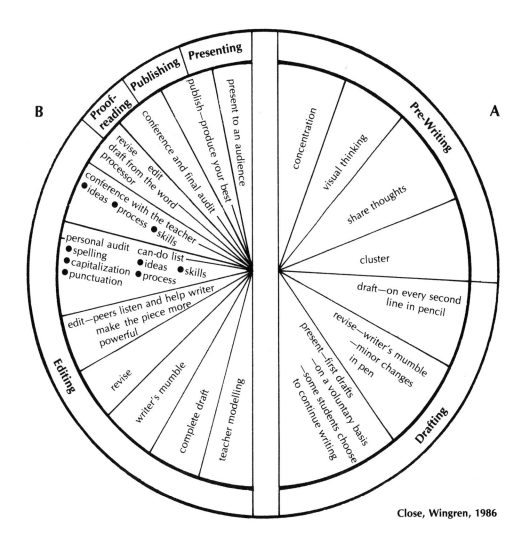

Close, Wingren, 1986

A. Expressive Writing
Students develop fluency by engaging in a systematic set of strategies that free them to express their thoughts in writing.

B. Writers' Workshop
Students choose a draft to publish. The drafts are taken through a series of steps to polish and present the ideas. Students engage in the same process as professional writers and illustrators.

The first half of the cycle is devoted to pre-writing and drafting. Strategies within each step enable all students to express their ideas with fluency and ease. They reach for language that matches their thinking.

A cornerstone to our interpretation of the writing process is the foundation of visual thinking and clustering as pre-writing strategies with young students. Six years ago we found our students' beginning attempts at writing weak. This is no longer so. Visual thinking puts the student in the position of "being there" in the simulated experience, allowing the student to think, speak, feel, and know from an insider's perspective. Clustering (Rico, 1983) is a tool to free thoughts and images. The associations children experience as they work with their own clusters and listen to other students' connections lead to the draft. In the act of composing, the text emerges. One line helps to create the next.

Students draft for many purposes and in response to many experiences — reading, speaking, listening, viewing, art, drama. Sometimes teachers will have the students leave their drafts for a length of time and then redraft to get closer to the intended meaning. Another time the teacher might have the students draft to reflect on a learning experience or to internalize content. The students might collect many drafts as they proceed through a learning unit, but only select a few to be published.

The second half of the cycle — editing, proofreading, publishing, and presenting — leads the students to express their thinking in form. Students craft thoughts in an editing process, use conventions of print in a proofreading process, and learn ways to publish and present their polished pieces.

As we explored writing as a process, we found parallels for reading as a process. The processes are inextricably connected. Working with the interdependence of the reading-writing processes, all of the stages can be driven by strategies that lead all students to higher thought and independent learning. By internalizing these strategies, students add tools to their developing tool kits.

Individual processing strategies guide the students to new learning. As students add strategies to their repertoires, they gain both confidence and a sense of independence.

Underlying this whole approach to learning is a fundamental respect for the individual and his or her role as a decision-maker in learning. Teachers and learners collaborate. Students learn to appreciate and to give appreciation. They learn to value both their contributions and those of others. Rotations through the processes of learning give the students confidence through developing competence. They want to know and understand as they become members in a club of learners. Learning is exhilarating for both teachers and students.

The Constructive Model of Learning

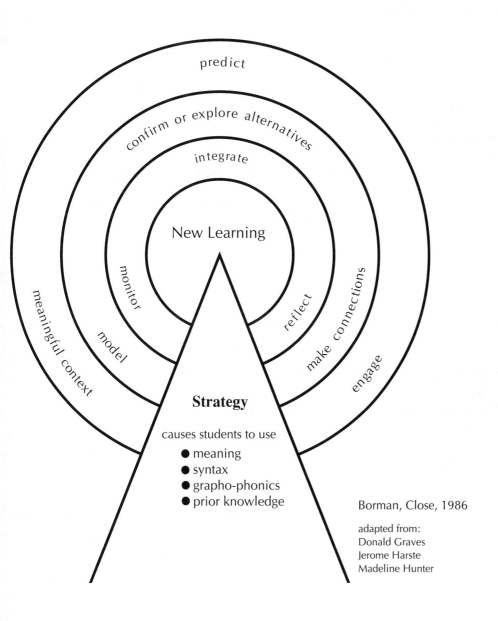

predict

confirm or explore alternatives

integrate

New Learning

meaningful context

monitor

model

reflect

make connections

engage

Strategy

causes students to use

● meaning
● syntax
● grapho-phonics
● prior knowledge

Borman, Close, 1986

adapted from:
Donald Graves
Jerome Harste
Madeline Hunter

Getting Started ● exploring possibilities

Pre-Reading

- activating schema and prior knowledge
- anticipating author's purpose for writing and establishing your purpose for reading
- establishing context for reader-writer dialogue
- predicting new learnings
- arousing curiosity

Pre-Writing

- playing with ideas
- preparing through simulation—leading to the development of voice
- networking thoughts
- shared student talk
- strengthening connections
- posing questions
- formulating hypotheses

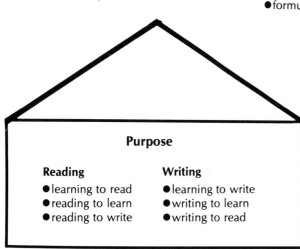

Purpose

Reading	**Writing**
● learning to read	● learning to write
● reading to learn	● writing to learn
● reading to write	● writing to read

The Reading - Writing Cycle

● Driven by strategies that lead students to higher thought and independent learning

Publishing -Presenting   ● sharing your polished thinking

Reading

- linking new learning to personal experience
- acknowledging new connections

Writing

- designing format
- celebrating the final copy

Drafting ●shaping thoughts

Comprehending

- making connections between author and reader
- matching voices
- predicting the author's thoughts
- confirming or rejecting the hypotheses
- exploring alternatives
- asking new questions
- forming new hypotheses
- making new connections
- re-defining and composing meanings
- reading aloud to "hear" message
- using punctuation, syntax, and context to assist meaning
- using spelling conventions to assist meaning
- experiencing unknown worlds
- identifying with new people and settings

Composing

- expressing personal voice in writing
- using language to match thought
- reflecting on learning experiences
- making new connections
- internalizing learning
- new thinking leads to deeper understanding
- re-writing text as purposes change or become defined
- re-reading aloud to "hear" meaning
- sharing drafts

SELECTED DRAFTS CONTINUE

Editing ●crafting thoughts

Reading

- checking your ideas out with the author's ideas
- substantiating from text
- reader-writer dialogue
- using what you know
- melding the known and the unknown
- re-reading parts as purpose is defined, clarified, or changed

Writing

- choosing form that matches purpose and audience
  - establishing criteria for the form
  - hearing models that reflect quality use of the form
  - adding criteria based on new knowledge
  - analyzing student writing based on criteria developed
- sculpting text — reaching again for language that matches thinking
- polishing ideas with others
- re-reading to "hear" message
- sharing what you did and why you did it

Proofreading ●using conventions of print

Reading

- validating the author's purpose

Writing

- establishing criteria for correct usage
- seeing models of conventions
- adding criteria based on new knowledge
- learning techniques to guide proof-reading — personal audit
- analyzing student writing based on criteria developed
- applying new knowledge to completed draft
- sharing what you know and how you use it

Image—Cluster—Draft

The foundation of powerful writing is ably using what you know in a creative, productive fashion. This Image—Cluster—Draft Strategy builds from the experience of the students in a whole-class lesson. Students begin by individually recording what they know in a learning log, then share these assumptions with a partner. The teacher reads a text, then an image of the text to provide opportunities for students to construct meaning. Students then cluster and draft on topic. The use of imagery and clustering prior to drafting heightens the power of the writing.

"Imagination is by far the most neglected and underdeveloped of the normal abilities of the human mind. It is the forgotten and rusting key to many treasures of the mind."

Barbara Brown, *Supermind*

"Clustering is a powerful inspirational/organizational tool; it always reassures us that we have something to say. Best of all, we don't have to worry about the sequence or syntax of ideas; we simply create connections and relationships as the cluster unfolds effortlessly."

Gabriele Lusser Rico, *Writing the Natural Way*

"The most powerful vehicle for change is the image; it is the central, pivotal part of mind."

Michael T. Bagley, *Imagery to Develop Memory*

"Research indicates that intelligence is directly related to multi-sensory processing (Galyean, 1980) and maximum retention over long term is greatly enhanced when all lobes of the brain are simultaneously stimulated...Imagery has been found to be the single most effective curriculum intervention strategy for simultaneously stimulating the four lobes of the brain because it involves mental stimulation of all the senses and kinesthetic body, higher level thinking skills, cognitive information to be processed, and a chance to respond emotionally as well as intellectually."

Karen Hess, *Enhancing Writing Through Imagery*

Classroom Story

TEACHER: "Today we are using a strategy called Image-Cluster-Draft. We will share our knowledge about owls, and listen to a poem about the great gray owl.(1) Then we will discuss owl facts and mental pictures the author's words made us see. After talking together we will use clusters to develop our ideas before we draft. This strategy is a tool. You can use it whenever you want to find out what you know and you can use it to connect information in new ways.(2) In your learning log write down everything you know about owls. I'll give you about two minutes.(3)

"Now turn to the person beside you and read what you wrote.

"Did any of you learn anything from your partner that you didn't know before?"(4)

STUDENTS: *"Owls regurgitate food to feed their young."*
"They can turn their necks completely around."
"Owls have good eyesight."
"After they've eaten they spit out fur and bones that are called pellets."
"Owls fly almost silently."

TEACHER: "Before we begin our study, what questions do you have about owls?"

STUDENTS: *"How many kinds of owls are there?"*
"How many babies do they have?"
"What enemies do they have?"

TEACHER: "Can anyone give possible answers to these questions?"(5)

STUDENTS: *"I know that there are snowy owls and barn owls and I'd like to know about other kinds too."*
"I think they have four or five babies."

TEACHER: "Are there any more questions?"

STUDENTS: *"How do they fly so silently?"*
"I once watched a show on Channel 9 that showed special feathers on the wing tips that help them."

TEACHER: "Now I'm going to read you the book we talked about, *The Great Gray Owl*, to show you how one author expresses his understanding of owls."

The teacher read two or three pages from *The Great Gray Owl* by Orin Cochrane.

TEACHER: "What do you see happening?"

Teacher Thoughts

(1) The teacher creates the context for learning.

(2) Sharing metacognition (thinking about thinking) with students allows students to understand the processes of learning.

(3) Students access stored information.

(4) Pooling information values each student's contribution and stimulates new thought.

(5) Formulating hypotheses sets a purpose for listening.

Teacher Thoughts

Classroom Story

STUDENTS: "I see me coming out of the hole in my tree. Bones are lying around on the branch."
"I can see a furry little mouse hiding in the grass. I can see his ears, legs, mostly everything."(6)

(6) Students orally reflect the details of the pictures the words helped them to create.

TEACHER: "What is life like for this owl?"

STUDENTS: "I think his life is easy. He catches what he wants. Other animals leave him alone."
"It's neat to fly. People can't do that."

The teacher read another two pages.

TEACHER: "What did these words make you think about?"

STUDENTS: "I saw a man with a glove and a string with an owl at the end that bites the string and flies away."
"I see a man waving his arm at the owl like a fist."

The teacher finished reading the book.

TEACHER: "What do you see life being like for the owl?"

STUDENTS: "Hard. People can go to the fridge. If an owl doesn't have good skills to catch food it wouldn't survive."
"And it does have enemies. Gangs of crows can kill owls."

TEACHER: "What words did the author use to help you make such a strong picture?"

From her Grade 5 class, the teacher collected powerful language samples and wrote them on the board.

STUDENTS: "Carnivorous."
"Night creatures."
"Killer from the sky."
"Merciless."(7)

(7) Vocabulary is taught in the context of a whole.

TEACHER: "What evidence do you have from the text that this creature was merciless?"

STUDENTS: "He devoured rodents with no feeling."
"I disagree because on one hand it might have to kill to survive but it was willing to share with its own babies."

Classroom Story

TEACHER: "What was this poem about?"(8)

> STUDENTS: *"Nature's way."*
> *"Owls."*
> *"The life cycle."*
> *"Great gray owl."*
> *"The food chain."*
> *"Cruelty."*
> *"Survival."*

TEACHER: "I'm going to read some words that will help your thinking about the gray owl. Put yourself into a comfortable thinking position."

The teacher waited a few seconds and then began to read her image. The words "thinking position" caused a quiet to settle in the room. Previously the students and teacher had reflected on what people looked like when they were thinking. Now students scratched their heads, put two hands to their chins, or closed their eyes. All were obviously concentrating.

> TEACHER:
> See yourself as the owl...(allow 2-3 seconds)
> Feel your talons grip the branch...
> Feel the breeze, cool...
> See the sun setting...
> See the shadows below...
> Feel the strength in your wings...
> Set off to hunt...
> Feel your eyes penetrate the dark...
> Soar...
> Hear a stir, far below...
> Drop from the sky...
> Dart at your prey...
> Grip...
> Fly off...
> Feed your young...
> Nestle together, tired...
> Sleep 'til night.

(9)

TEACHER: "I want you to stay with the picture you've created for another minute or so. Talk in your mind about what you are seeing... hearing... feeling... noticing...(10)

"Now turn to a person near you and share what you were thinking. Feel free to ask each other questions."

Students talked animatedly for two to three minutes. (11)

TEACHER: "Would anyone like to share their thinking with the whole group?"

> STUDENTS: *"I see the owl as an omnipotent creature threatening the night sky."*

Teacher Thoughts

(8) By discussing the essence of the text, students develop the big picture. This sharing brings the parts back to the whole.

(9) Image works when you get close to the act by using simple language, allowing the students to fill in their own details.

(10) This further processing step allows the imagers to evoke and control their own images.

(11) Articulating thinking makes new connections and clarifies understanding.

Teacher Thoughts

Classroom Story

"I don't see why people get upset with what owls do, 'cause we don't start to cry when we eat a steak."
"I'm the ruler of the night." (12)

(12) Hearing possibilities makes for more associations in each learner's mind.

TEACHER: "See yourself as the owl. Put the word 'owl' in a circle in the middle of your paper. Begin clustering what life is like for the great gray owl." (13)

(13) Clustering allows associations to pour out and the mind to perceive patterns effortlessly.

The students clustered until a natural break was sensed three to four minutes later. While they clustered, the teacher wrote on the blackboard.

TEACHER: "Look at the words in your cluster. Circle ones you find powerful. Draw lines between words that connect for any reason. It doesn't have to make sense to anyone else. There is no right or wrong way to cluster. When you feel ready, begin writing. Show what life is like as an owl." (14)

(14) Extended prewriting fills students' minds with both images and facts.

Students began writing. The teacher drafted, again on the blackboard, modelling revisions as her thinking changed. After four or five minutes she stopped.

TEACHER: "Does anyone want to share their beginning?"

STUDENTS: *"The last of the sunlight sinks below the bounds of sight."*
"Graceful wings spread wide."
"The wind ruffled my feathers as I flew over my forest, feeling very proud of my territory."
"My cramped wings slowly opened and stretched."
"Every day I do the same things."
"I was just waking up as the sun began to set and I could sense the moisture of the dew beginning to set on the grass." (15)

(15) Students have internalized knowledge in a way that allows them to write with authority.

The children returned to their writing for another five or six minutes.

TEACHER: "Now let's read out loud what we've written so far. Writers do this to see if their writing makes sense. As you hear your words, be thinking, 'Is that what I really want to say?' We'll call this the 'writer's mumble.'

"Did anyone make changes?" (16)

(16) Students see that language is not fixed just because it is written. Language can be changed to best fit the intended meaning.

STUDENT: *"I wrote, 'As I peered down at the sleeping forest below, I loosened my steel-like grip.' "*

TEACHER: "Why did you do that?"

STUDENT: *"It makes it sound more real."*

Classroom Story

Teacher Thoughts

TEACHER: "Did anyone else make changes?"

    STUDENT: "*I left the first sentence the same but changed the second one. My second sentence was 'I pull my wings beating on the wind.' I changed it to 'I pull my wings in and swoop.'*"

TEACHER: "We're going to start sharing some of our drafts now. If you wish more time please continue." (17)

(17) Satisfaction and celebration of shaped thought reinforces the importance of oral communication.

As the presenting of first drafts ended, the teacher reflected with her students.

TEACHER: "What did we do first today?" (18)

(18) Reflecting on the process helps students internalize knowledge.

    STUDENT: "*We wrote down what we knew about owls.*"

TEACHER: "Why did we do that?"

    STUDENTS: "*To share what we know.*"
    "*To give each other ideas.*"

TEACHER: "What else did we do?"

    STUDENTS: "*We listened to a poem about owls.*"
    "*We talked about what the words made us think of.*"
    "*Then we clustered.*"

TEACHER: "What else did we do?"

    STUDENTS: "*We wrote, trying to show what an owl's life is like.*"
    "*I wasn't sure how to start. When I heard Kelly's beginning, I got an idea. The words raced out of my head.*"

TEACHER: "What happened when we used this strategy?"

    STUDENTS: "*I was surprised because I didn't know I knew so much about owls.*"
    "*Talking gave me all kinds of new ideas.*"
    "*I felt like I was there, so it was easy to write.*"

TEACHER: "Did anyone else feel like Kevin? (19) What did you notice about the drafts today?"

(19) Many hands went up.

    STUDENTS: "*There weren't any extra words.*"
    "*They were all different.*"

Teacher Thoughts

Classroom Story

TEACHER: "That makes it very special, doesn't it, when we can express our ideas our own way. Each time we write we find new ways to say things. Do you have any new questions about owls?"

STUDENTS: "I wonder if they really sleep out on a branch?"
"What are those balls owls spit?"
"How do they digest food?"

TEACHER: "Tomorrow we'll be seeing a film about owls and we'll use a different strategy to learn more."

Before Teaching

I know   Kellie

Owls are night time birds. They sleep during the day, and hunt at night. Owls are generally very wise. They have good eyesight so they can see in the dark. She hunt mice, moles etc. They swoop down to catch them then eat them. When they have eaten them they spit out the bones and fur which are called pelts. There are several different type of owls. Such as Snowy owls which are small and white.

DRAFT

Cluster after Teaching

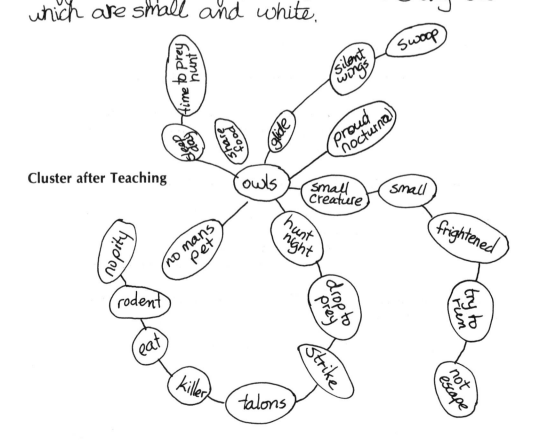

As I slowly wake up I'm hungry so are my owlets I venture out on my hunt. As I am flying through the air I see a small mouse scurrying along the field below. I speed up, then swoop down, my sharp talons grab ~~the mouse~~ him. Then I stop, the mouse is dead I eat it. Feeling proud, When I am ~~done~~ down I cough back the flesh, fur, and bones. Again I start my flight for food this time to find something for my babies. I am the ruler of the night. I will find something.

DRAFT

Extensions

1. The teacher had her students use the learning logs to record new knowledge about owls. The initial questions triggered research. She took the class into the library. They worked in groups of three searching through resources. As they found facts, she had them record each fact on a separate flashcard. Later they categorized the findings, made concept maps, and wrote again using the image—cluster—draft strategy. The students were writing to reflect on their learning. At the end of the unit, she had them turn their knowledge into a letter. Only the letter was taken on to publishing.

2. To create a cluster, begin with a word circled in the middle of a page. That central word will make you think of a new word or phrase. Write your thoughts quickly, each in its own circle, radiating outward from the centre in any direction. Connect each word or phrase with a line to the preceding circle. When something new or different strikes you, begin again at the centre and radiate outward until those associations are exhausted. After three to five minutes, or when you feel your associations are finished, take a minute to circle powerful words and to connect words that seem to go together. (These ideas are adapted from *Writing the Natural Way* by Gabriele Lusser Rico.) Move right on to a piece of drafting paper and begin writing.

   If any of your students seem reluctant to begin writing, tell them it's important to get the pencil moving on the paper. You might suggest that they just write again until a flow of thought begins. Another approach is to have the students sketch briefly and then write. Prior to drafting, students in early primary classrooms always sketch before writing. In Kindergarten and early Grade 1, we have the students cluster in pictures. When they are ready, they move naturally into clustering with invented spelling.

After discussing what writers do when they don't know how to spell a word, teachers model writing on the blackboard. We help the students to see that writers invent spellings to show what they mean. The teacher modelling on the blackboard frees the students to experiment with language. When they see the teacher crossing out words and making changes, they also begin to revise. A serious tone blankets the room. Students need to know that spelling is a proofreading skill, and writers focus on spelling after their thinking has been shaped. We are very careful not to devalue any approximation.

When students standardize the spelling for publication, they celebrate how many of the letters they got right in a word. The teacher might say, ''Look at what you can do, John. You got four out of seven letters right. Tell us what you were thinking as you spelled that word.'' Hearing how others try to spell develops a spelling consciousness in the students. After the students try to spell the word the teacher might say, ''This is the way it is spelled in a book.''

3.   Teachers often wonder how this individual student writing looks in a Grade 1 classroom. Some teachers have found the structure of a cluster worksheet helps them move toward students freely clustering. Others begin the first day of school with a blank page. Students move through the same sequence of teacher-directed activities, but choose either to draw or use invented spelling to represent their thinking in a cluster.

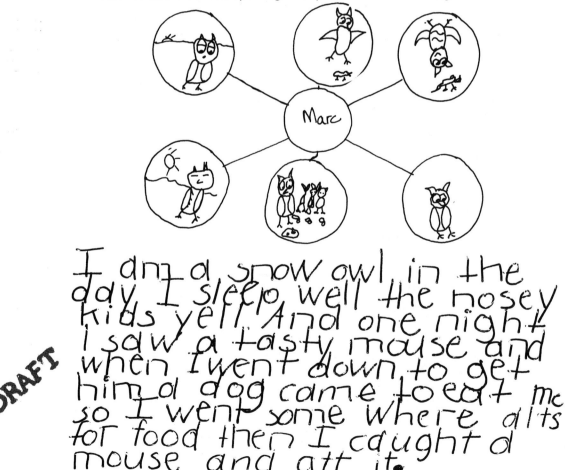

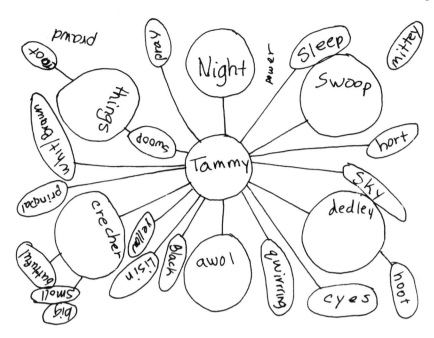

I am a a owol and I am
looking fore a mouse
because I am very hungrey.
I don't like peiopol feeding
me because I like the taste
of my one food more than
other food. So I go out
and get my one food. wen I see
a mouse I swoop down and I
sneek up and I get the mouse with
my dedly clos. I carey the mouse in
my pawoforl beck I carey the mouse
to my holl in my holl I eat the mouse
then I fly above looking for a
plase to rest. I rest on the
soft hay. I wat in tell day then
I slep ther.

4. In kindergarten some children may begin to experiment with words on
    paper. Children demonstrate their knowledge in many different ways and
    with varying degrees of sophistication.

CHaRLene Br B+ Ahd
Didit sAy Atsusme

*Charlene burped and
didn't say excuse me.*

DRAFT

Once upon a time there was a bear who fell in love with the moon and he loved the moon so much that he started to think and that night he put some honey to feed the moon and the birds ate it.

5. The language of imagery is new to many of us. Many teachers have found *200 Ways of Using Imagery in the Classroom* by Michael T. Bagley and Karen Hess and *Enhancing Writing Through Imagery* by Karen Hess useful books to guide them with specific examples for free writing and writing in the content areas.

6. Any curricular activity can be heightened through the use of imagery. After a field trip or a science experiment, or after reading to students, the teacher might consolidate the learning by leading the students through an image.

The teacher creates a bare-bones sketch of the actual experience, using key words like see...feel...hear...notice.... Giving as few details as possible allows the students to fill in from their own experience. At the end of the imaging, students sit quietly for a minute or two. The teacher directs them to stay with the image they have created, silently talking to themselves about what they see. Writing appears stronger with the inclusion of this final step.

To help students understand the concept of the electric circuit, the following image could be used:

The Life of an Electron

See yourself as a tiny electron at one side of a battery, the zinc electrode...
Feel full of energy, trapped on this side...
Notice the murky acidic space...
Feel a wire connecting to your electrode...
See the wire leading to a light bulb and onto the carbon electrode on the other side of the battery...
Feel yourself being pushed out to freedom...
Notice millions of electrons bumping on the pathway...
See a tungsten coil inside a lightbulb just ahead...
Feel the strain as you move around the coil...
Notice your energy drain...
Look back...
Understand that your energy helped light the bulb...
Feel the radiated heat...
Feel yourself revitalized at the carbon electrode...

Adapted from a metaphor written by Langley science teacher Susan Kovach.

Recipe
Image—Cluster—Draft

1. Read an image to students.

2. Ask students to share the images from their minds with the people beside them.

3. Individually, students cluster from the image.

4. Individually, students circle powerful words in their clusters and draw lines to connect words in their clusters.

5. Begin writing.

6. Share beginnings.

7. Continue writing.

8. Do a writer's mumble.

9. Share drafts.

10. Reflect on process with students.

Clustering from Text

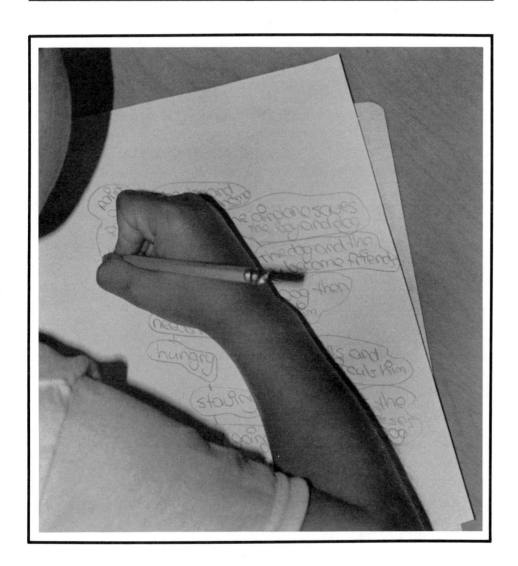

The Clustering from Text strategy facilitates students making connections with new knowledge, based on the reader/writer relationship. While the teacher reads a piece of informational text, students privately create images. These are shared in a group cluster, then re-organized to deepen connections and further socially construct meaning. On a re-reading of text, students create personal clusters, then write in role. This powerful strategy integrates the learner's personal knowledge with the collective knowledge and understandings of the group. Curriculum grows from the learners' experiences.

"Deep processing is consciously generating these parts of a thought: the mental pictures, linguistic information, sensory information and feelings. It is actively creating experiences for each of the different aspects of a thought. When you deep process, you take a thought and artificially expand it so that it has all of the components listed above."

Robert J. Marzano and Daisy E. Arredondo,
Tactics for Thinking

"Clustering is a self-organizing process. As you spill out seemingly random words and phrases around a centre, you will be surprised to see patterns forming until a moment comes - characterized by an 'aha' feeling - when you suddenly sense a focus for writing."

Gabriele Lusser Rico, *Writing the Natural Way*

"Our students need to postpone writing until their information begins to coalesce into ideas, and until they feel a sense of authority. Then they need to write."

Lucy McCormick Calkins, *The Art of Teaching Writing*

"Our brains are attuned to the subleties of voice, intonation and pauses. According to Joseph C. Pearce, a student of brain processes, sound - and particularly vocal sound - stimulates the brain into attention."

Gabriele Lusser Rico, *Writing the Natural Way*

Classroom Story

TEACHER: "We are going today to do some listening and writing and, most importantly, sharing our thinking. To do this, I will read you a poem. While I am reading the poem, I want you to let your minds relax and see what pictures or images come to you. When I have finished reading, we will share our images. You may want to close your eyes to help your mind make pictures while I read. Be sure you have a comfortable spot where you won't interfere with someone else's thinking."

The children in the Grade 2 class wiggled into comfortable positions. Most closed their eyes as the teacher's voice began Orin Cochrane's poem.

TEACHER: "My poem is called *The Great Gray Owl*. As I read I will not be showing you the pictures that the illustrator chose because I want your minds to be free to make your own pictures. (1)

> Wake
>> Mighty owl
>> For the sun has set
>> Proud nocturnal creature
>> You are no man's pet.

"All right, open your eyes. Please share with me any pictures that came as you were listening. Together we will make a cluster."

She drew an oval on the board but placed no word in it. (2)

STUDENT: *"Owl."*

She joined "owl" to the oval and circled the word.

STUDENT: *"Night."*

TEACHER: "I am going to be your hands. You need to do all the thinking and tell my hands where to place your words. Should I attach 'night' to 'owl' or to the empty circle?" (3)

STUDENTS: *"To 'owl' because owls fly at night."*
" 'Moon' by 'night.' "
" 'Hunt' by 'moon.' They hunt at night."
" 'House' by 'owl.' It's where it lives."
" 'Creek' by the house. That's where I saw it." (4)

The sharing continued. The children built quickly from one another's images and made several chains emanating from "owl."

STUDENT: *" 'Share' - I think put it separate."*

TEACHER: "Why do you choose to put 'share' on a new chain?"

No response.

"Can someone help Erica with her thinking? Why would she choose to put 'share' on a new chain?"

Teacher Thoughts

(1) Children develop stronger images when they use their own thought rather than refine someone else's images. However, with K-1 children, the text is frequently a big book. In this case, the additional use of the pictures as clues to reading is helpful.

(2) If the teacher leaves the circle blank, students can make their own choices for a key word. Placing a centre word at this stage limits thinking.

(3) The question asks for instructions based on a thinker's decisions but does not impose the teacher's rules for organizing knowledge.

(4) All responses are accepted. We are helping to organize children's thinking, not evaluating it.

Teacher Thoughts

Classroom Story

STUDENTS: *"Because it's what the owl does with her babies."*
"Because it's different. It's not like night."

TEACHER: "Thank you. Erica, could you agree with that thinking? O.K. It really helps our minds work well when we build on each other's ideas." (5)

(5) Other students extend the volunteer's response. The ownership for placement of the word rests with the original respondent.

STUDENTS: *" 'Listen' - separate. Because owls listen and share."*
" 'Trees' - by itself."
" 'Nest' - to 'trees.' That's where the nest is."

TEACHER: "My, did you notice how well you are building on each other's ideas? As soon as I wrote down 'trees,' half of your hands shot up. John's image really sparked your thinking, didn't it? I think he helped your minds form new ideas." (6)

(6) Teachers build metacognitive awareness of the thinking process, even with young children.

She continued collecting words from the children. They were exuberant sharers and keenly listened to each other. As the ideas began to ebb, and her chart paper filled, she changed course.

TEACHER: "Wow! You are really a group of fluent thinkers. My hands could hardly keep up. Now I want you to have your minds change channels. Look at our cluster. Notice how we made chains of associations or

Classroom Story

Teacher Thoughts

thoughts that linked together. There are many ways these words can be joined. I want you to see if you can see new ways to join words in this cluster. Please tell me your reasons for joining. Once again I'll be your hands and just mark down your thinking." (7)

(7) Reorganization of the cluster deepens thinking and links new connections.

The children studied the cluster, then began to share their new associations. The teacher circled words and joined them in a second colour. They evidently enjoyed this activity. Their thinking was very sophisticated. She encouraged and extended the thinking at every opportunity, clarifiying and linking student to student, image to image.

STUDENTS: " 'Babies' and 'eggs' because they come from eggs."
"They hatch. Join 'hatch' too."
" 'Thunder' and 'fright. 'When it thunders out, I'm scared!"
" 'Trees' and 'play.' Owls play in trees."
" We need to add 'branches.' The nest is in the branches." (8)

(8) Again, all responses are accepted. Thinking is being shared. To promote a risk-free enivronment, all thought is honoured.

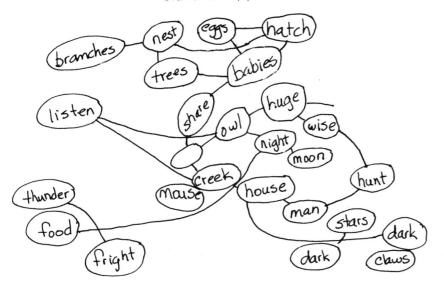

The excitement of the almost limitless possibilities of new connections flourished. She wove several more together, then gave new directions.

Teacher Thoughts

(9) Children need an opportunity to make a personal commitment.

(10) This looking at the world through someone else's eyes helps create a personal voice for writing.

(11) By interviewing children prior to having them write, more extensions are built from shared student talk.

Classroom Story

TEACHER: "You have listened and thought very well together. I want you to save your good ideas because you will be able to use them in just a moment. On your desk is a piece of paper. I want you to draw a circle and put in it a word that will help your mind flow with ideas. It will be your private choice. (9) Next I will read the poem again, and as I read I want you to make your own cluster of images that come to you from our poem.

"Think about who you would be if you were inside the poem and what life would be like for you. (10) Keep it a secret. We will share some of these private thoughts after."

She read and the children rapidly began personal clusters. They seemed to reflectively collect and arrange their words as she read.

TEACHER: "Add just a couple more words to your cluster. Be thinking of who you are and what life is like for you.

"Who are you?" (11)

STUDENT: "I'm a mouse."

TEACHER: "What's life like for you?"

STUDENT: "It's scary. I have to go and get food for my babies and this owl keeps chasing me."

TEACHER: "Yes, that would be scary. Who are you?"

STUDENTS: "I'm the owl. I'm big and strong and I swoop down on mices!"
"I'm a star. I twinkle and watch everything happening."
"I'm the grass. It's horrible. Everybody steps on me except the owl. He flies over me."

TEACHER: "Turn your papers over. Tell me your story of who you are and what life is like for you. You may choose to be who you shared with us, or you may now have another idea. Perhaps you could start with 'I am' and then I'll know who you are right at the beginning."

Papers flipped. The only sounds in the class were sounds of writers at work. After twenty minutes, they stopped to do a writer's mumble.

TEACHER: "Let's do a writer's mumble before we do some sharing. We all read together, quietly out loud to ourselves. This helps us find something we might have missed in our writing because our brains were going so fast on ideas.

"Great! Now who would like to share their early draft?"

Classroom Story

The writing was brilliant - deep, personal interpretation of text, written in a strong, consistent voice. The power of these children's shared thoughts was astounding. (12)

I'm mad, I'm Mad becuase my branches are brockin and I'm All scrached up, I hate being a bush. It's hard to kep my leaves on. All the owl's come swoPing down into me, I hate being a bush beccdase mice alwys run into me and hert me that's knot all I hate being a bush becuase men alwy's shute at owl's som times they mise and shute me That's the Worst thing But somtimes I like being A bush becuase people take care of me. The End

Teacher Thoughts

(12) Children have far exceeded our expectations in their use of sophisticated language. All levels of experience with print blend to create personal meaning at increasingly skilled levels.

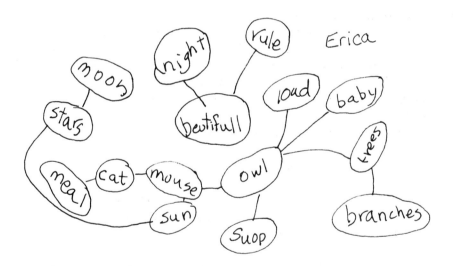

Extensions

"Look and see is not enough. Appreciating a work of art demands intelligent application of perceptual and cognitive resources."
        David Perkins, "Art as an Occasion of Intelligence,"
        Educational Leadership, Vol. 45, No. 4, 1988

One of Richmond's Teacher Consultants, Donna Gilchrist, has adapted this strategy to use with images. She explains her extension as follows:

> In literature, the clustering of images comes from the text
> that is read to the students. In art, the clustering of thoughts or
> key words comes from the image that students view. The art im-
> age is another vehicle that speaks to the viewer about emotions,

experiences, places, and people in time, and scenes in the artist's imagination. Images show a variety of ways of viewing the world we live in. Students will view a picture for representation and expression. Older students will look for symbolism as well. The clustering technique is very similar to that used with a text. The teacher would do the following while working with a class:

1. Display an image that can be viewed easily by all students. Allow two to three minutes of quiet viewing time. Encourage the students to involve all their senses while viewing - what could you see? hear? smell? taste? and feel (emotionally too)?

2. Ask students *objectively* to share the thoughts that came to their minds as they viewed the image.

3. Record the thoughts in a group cluster. Have the students direct where each idea is placed, i.e. if they want their word linked to a previous circle or to stand alone to start a new cluster.

4. As you record, circle the words and draw connecting lines. Have the student explain how the words connect and why.

5. As the thinking slows, redirect the students to make new connections. "Can you show new ways to join the words?" Record these in a different colour and ask for explanations as to how and why the words connect.

6. Have students make individual clusters. Students can *remain* with the image or move *outside* the image to a personal thought.

7. As the *students cluster*, individually check their levels of thinking through explanation of how and why words are joined.

8. Have the students *draw* the ideas that they have clustered. Students may choose the whole cluster or just a chain to include in their own *draft* picture.

9. Have the students *draft* a story about the picture they have drawn.

10. *Share* their pictures and stories.

This is a very brief outline of clustering from an image. From my own experience, here are some additional thoughts to consider when using the teaching strategy:

objectivity - This is critical as it encourages students to express themselves freely. There is no fear of not pleasing the teacher. A teacher's preferences/prejudices will bias and narrow student thinking.

remain - If the students remain with the image, their writing and pictures will be directly related to the image.

outside - If the students choose to go outside the image, their writing and pictures will be linked to the image only through the single thought that each student had chosen to initiate his or her personal cluster.

In both of the above choices, the teacher may want to narrow the choice; the image may also help to determine the style of writing.

students cluster - Some students will need assistance in this form of thinking. Guide by asking questions to clarify their own thought processes and showing possible solutions, not "the answer."

draw - Have each student use a coloured marker, pen, or pencil crayon to draw a *draft*. As in writing, the drawing process also includes a rough trial of working out on paper one's own images. The use of a permanent marker aids in the drafting process by not allowing the students to erase but rather to incorporate all ideas - mistakes too!

draft - The teacher at this point should decide if the draft is to go to publication quality or be left as a draft. This will vary depending on teacher purpose.

share - As with presenting stories, each student should be able to talk about his or her picture with respect to what he or she likes about it and why.

Working with the clustering strategy provides the teacher with another tool for eliciting thoughts from students.

Recipe
Clustering from Text

1. Read a passage of text to your students. Encourage them to form images in their minds as they listen to the text.

2. Ask them to share the images or pictures that came to their minds as you read.

3. As they share, record the images in a group cluster. Have the students direct where each suggestion goes, i.e., if they want their words linked to previous words or if they want to start new chains.

4. As you record, circle the words and draw connecting lines. Have the student explain how the words connect and why.

5. Once the thinking has slowed, redirect the students to make new connections. "Can you think of other ways to connect these words?" Have students elaborate on these new connections they are making. Record these in a different colour.

6. Read the text a second time.

7. As you read, have students make individual clusters. You can encourage students to remain inside or outside the text.

8. As they are listening and clustering, they should also address, "Who are you in this selection and what is life like for you?"

9. Share the personal choices.

10. Continue clustering or immediately begin to draft their written responses to the text, "Who are you and what is life like for you?"

Brainstorm—Categorize

    Effective teachers support the learning that is already in place. With the Brainstorm—Categorize Strategy, teachers, prior to a unit of study, collect and categorize students' prior knowledge on the unit. As the class collectively categorized students' prior knowledge, shared group knowledge extends students' learning and prepares students for the unit. Reader response is heightened as students seek out clarification and support for evidence generated in the group work.

"We are unable to learn anything we cannot relate to something we know, to some meaning we already have. It is only through the interrelationships of concepts or categories that anything has meaning. The interrelationships are the basis of our entire cognitive system, our theory of the world."

Ethel Buchanan, editor, *For the Love of Reading*

"If you use a text that will offer both opportunity and challenge to each child in the class then the related activities must ensure that the child interact with and manipulate the language of that text. By doing so, some of the author's language will come under the learner's control. Thus, the learner's language capacity is enhanced."

Terry D. Johnson and Daphne R. Louis, *Literacy Through Literature*

"To educate means to 'lead out' what each person carries within. And possibilities are all that is carried within."

Luis Alberto Machado, *The Right to Be Intelligent*

"...learning to read or proficient reading comprehension is an interactive process that takes place as the reader interprets the text. This interpretation is based on the experience and background of each child. You have to help your students to develop knowledge and experiences that will enhance their reading. One way to develop this background is through instruction in concept formation. In helping children learn how to form concepts, you are helping them to develop their critical thinking skills."

Diane Lapp and James Flood, "Promoting Reading Comprehension: Instruction Which Ensures Continuous Reader Growth." In *Promoting Reading Comprehension*, James Flood, editor.

Classroom Story

TEACHER: "We're going to be using a strategy called Brainstorm—Categorize. First we'll brainstorm what we know about owls and then we'll take these ideas and build categories together. Let's see what we already know and then later we'll look back. It'll be interesting to find out where we started and compare that list with what we know when we finish our owl study. (1)

"Before we brainstorm ideas, four secretaries are needed. Each will record the words in one section, as I record them on the board. (2) You'll notice this blackboard is divided into four sections where the words we generate about owls will be recorded."

1.	2.	3.	4.

Four volunteers were chosen by the teacher. Each was given supplies: a felt pen and a stack of manila tag cards.

TEACHER: "Secretaries, please print fairly large and have only one idea on each card. Sometimes a few words will have to be scrunched up a little to get them all on.

"You needn't wait and raise your hand in this part of the activity as long as we can hear one another easily. Just call out words at a speed that we can record them."

 STUDENT: *"Owls are big."*

The teacher recorded on the blackboard in Section 1.

The student secretary for Section 1 printed "big" in felt on one card.

TEACHER: "What else do we know about owls?"

 STUDENT: *"They like to eat rodents."*

1. big	2. eat rodents	3.	4.

Teacher Thoughts

(1) Prior to a new unit of study, students are empowered by recognizing what they already know.

(2) Students share in leadership positions. The blackboard records group knowledge. The cards facilitate concept formation.

Teacher Thoughts

Classroom Story

The teacher recorded in Section 2. The student secretary printed "eat rodents" on a card.

TEACHER: "Other things we know?"

     STUDENT: _"They hunt and eat their prey."_

Teacher recorded in Section 3. Student secretary for Section 3 printed "hunt" in felt pen on one card.

1 big	2. eat rodents	3. hunt	4.

Students began to warm to the activity and a flood of facts about owls inundated the furiously printing secretaries and teacher!

     STUDENTS: _"They can fly." (3)_
                    "They have babies."
                    "They catch moles and take them back to the tree."
                    "They have small brains."
                    "They sleep in the day and hunt at night."
                    "They have tiny heads."
                    "They fly quietly."
                    "That's because they have special feathers curved a certain way."
                    "Usually one baby is left in the nest and it dies."
                    "They have five to six babies."
                    "No, I heard on a nature show it's four to five."

(3) All student responses are accepted. Wrong information is later corrected as knowledge is refined.

TEACHER: "How about we'll put four to six and find out what's right later?"

     STUDENTS: _"Sure. They're cute, especially the owlettes."_
                    "They live in barns."
                    "Owls are all over the globe."

1. big	2. eat rodents	3. hunt	4. fly
have babies	catch moles	small brains	sleep in day
hunt at night	tiny heads	fly quietly	special feathers
one baby dies	4-6 babies	very cute	live in barns
all over globe			

Classroom Story

Teacher Thoughts

TEACHER: "You already know a lot about owls. That will help you when you start reading for further information. Have you noticed when you read that starting with some ideas about the subject already makes it easier to understand?"

STUDENTS: *"It does for me. And I like it when I read stuff I already know and I can say I told it to you and the class before."*
"Lots of times we know interesting things that the book doesn't tell. My dad takes me to the Science and Technology Center. I got to cut up an owl pellet and see bits of a mouse. They don't have bones in our science book." (4)

(4) Students bring personal meaning to content.

The class muttered questions about what the mouse bits were like. (5)

(5) Information that students wonder about can be placed in a separate "I wonder" category.

TEACHER: "Good. Our next look at these facts you came up with is to sort them into categories. We're interested in your thinking, just why you decided to put a certain word or group of words into the category. Since the word is yours when it's given to you, the final decision about which category it will stay in will be yours. However, I'd like you to explore other students' thinking too. Ask for advice before you settle on a category, and ask those students who give you advice to tell why they think one category makes more sense to them than another.

"Let's see how this works. We've passed out the cards so each of you has one. There are five pieces of masking tape on the board, one for each category we'll make up. Janice, what card do you have?" (6)

(6) Teacher controls the speed of sharing to enable all students to hear the speaker's thinking and to offer personal extensions.

Janice went to the front of the class and read "sleeps by day" and held up her card.

STUDENTS: *"I think I'll put it here and call it the 'domestic category.' Does anyone have advice?"*
"I think you should call it the 'sleeping category.' "
"I think the 'beginning category.' "
"I think it's a 'family category,' like all the things all owls to."

Janice agreed with the last advice she got and decided to call it "the family category." She chose Cindy to come up next. Cindy's card was "small brain."

STUDENTS: *"I'm calling 'small brain' a new category called 'small things' cause an owl's brain's in its small head."*
"Does anyone have any advice?"
"I think it could be in a category about how smart or dumb owls are."

Teacher Thoughts

Classroom Story

"What about a gentle category?"
"I think it's small things about owls, too."

Cindy agreed that she liked small things about owls best and didn't change her original thinking. The children now had the idea of the exercise and increased their suggestions. The next student selected "about babies" as a new category, followed by "4-5 babies."

(7) Student thinking is driving the language as it is being generated in discussion.

When "cute" came up, the student first decided on a new category but, with advice, decided cute described owl babies best and moved it. Some students clapped as it was moved. (7) "They live in barns" was thought to be a family category first but with advice the student agreed that it wasn't the only place owls could live so it didn't describe all of them. "They live in barns" then started a new category. Some students thought this should be in the family category but it remained in "homes." Some students also wanted a unique or "very special things about owls" category. The owner of the card "special feathers" decided to have a vote. The weight was in favour of moving "special feathers" to start another category, and it was done. (8)

(8) Duplicate cards can be made when consensus cannot be reached on the appropriate category. Students see thought having many connections and different perspectives.

An additional challenge arose. One student's card read "all over the world." He tried to add it to the category called "homes."

TEACHER: "I wonder if we could call this category something else to include this word? Does anyone have an idea?"

The class consensus was a change in category title to "where they live." (9)

(9) Category names must be written in chalk in order to grow and change with expanding student concepts.

Classroom Story   **Teacher Thoughts**

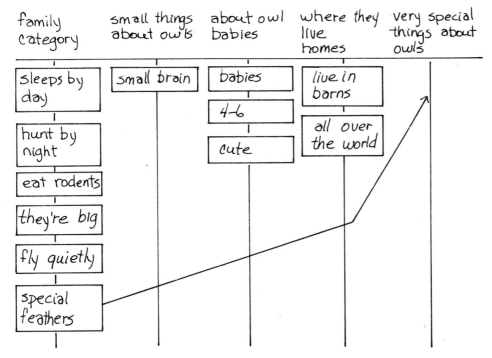

family category	small things about owls	about owl babies	where they live homes	very special things about owls
sleeps by day	small brain	babies	live in barns	
hunt by night		4-6	all over the world	
eat rodents		cute		
they're big				
fly quietly				
special feathers				

The exercise generated a lot of talking and listening. I could see classes, with practice, sustaining their attention, becoming masterful lawyer-like persuaders.

TEACHER: "It's time to finish. Was this a useful way for you to start thinking about owls today?" (10)

(10) Reflecting on learning is one of the most powerful ways of expanding thinking.

STUDENTS: "Yes."
"I wanted to just start finding out about pellets and what you can see that's left of the mouse." (11)
"I thought it's fun to hear how everyone thinks."

(11) Students have begun to anticipate the new information of the unit.

TEACHER: "How is that useful?"

STUDENT: "Well, it makes me kind of take their idea seriously and think some more about what I thought first."

TEACHER: "So you think one mind is sometimes helped by hearing other minds' thoughts?"

STUDENT: "Yeah, I do."

TEACHER: "Who agrees with that? You learn by listening hard to others' ideas."

STUDENTS: "And it's interesting, it's not so boring."
"I learned there's lots of ways to think about the

Teacher Thoughts

Classroom Story

same ideas and sometimes we can agree on a best way and sometimes we can't. Sometimes no one way seems better than another."

TEACHER: "Thank you for your respectful listening to each other. When we use this brainstorm—categorize strategy, what is most important is hearing each other's thinking. You did that most successfully."

(12) New connections are tied to prior knowledge and learning is extended.

The teacher made a bulletin board of the categories arranged under "what we know." As the unit on owls unfolded, I could picture the list growing with new learning about owls. (12)

Extensions

Teachers use this strategy in many different ways:

— after clustering from text to tap what students know before beginning a unit

— to show students what they know part way through a unit

— to reflect at the end of a learning experience

— for individual groups to generate possibilities, organize categories, and present their thinking to a class

— to access memory in a test situation by brainstorming what they know and categorizing their ideas

— to image words from the categories, cluster, and draft

— in Kindergarten and early Grade 1, teachers are categorizing with pictures

— in Grade 1 classes, the teacher records on cards on the blackboard. Cards are then distributed to the students and recategorized.

Recipe
Brainstorm—Categorize

1. Prepare board and strips of masking tape.

2. Select four students to record on cards.

3. Brainstorm topic, teacher recording words on board, four students printing words on cards.

4. Distribute cards to the class.

5. Categorize words, student by student, on the masking tape.

6. Encourage students to seek advice for categorizing from the class.

7. Discuss all requests for advice.

8. Change category names as required.

9. Save cards for recategorizing or use as graphic organizer.

Sort and Predict

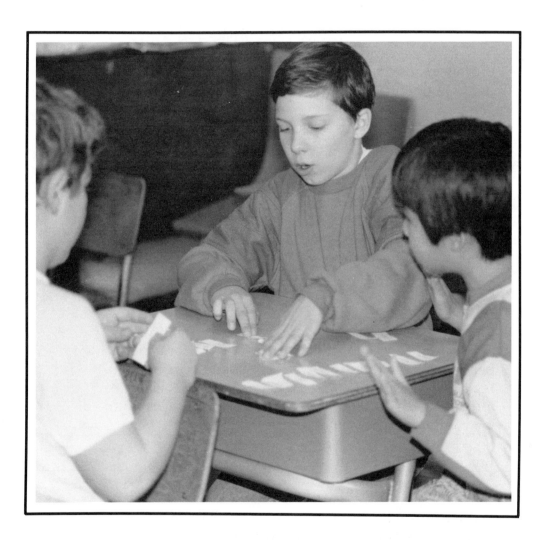

The Sort and Predict strategy has been proven to be very effective in primary through to secondary classrooms when the meaning of the text is closely tied to vocabulary knowledge. The teacher isolates approximately twenty words from the text and has small, mixed-ability groups of students arrange these words into categories. The talk and decision-making surrounding the categorization enable students to draw on their prior knowledge of the words and to link their meaning to that of others in their group. Students hypothesize what they will learn from the text once the sorting has been completed.

"Perhaps the most important of the new findings is the role of prior knowledge in reading comprehension. It is now well established that prior knowledge is one of the most powerful influences on how well a reader comprehends."

Paul T. Wilson, Richard C. Anderson, and Linda G. Fielding, *Children's Book Reading Habits: A New Criterion for Literacy*

"...guided activities help students learn to draw on their prior knowledge (Langer 1984) or autobiographical experience (Petrosky 1982) in making inferences. By connecting related knowledge or experiences to the text, students can activate schema that help them better understand the text."

Richard Beach, "Strategic Teaching in Literature." In *Strategic Teaching and Learning: Cognitive Instruction in the Content Areas*, Beau Fly Jones, Annemarie Sullivan Palincsar, Donna Sederburg Ogle, Eileen Glenn Carr, editors.

"...the process of forming concepts enabled the students to develop mental structures that held the information better than structures that were provided to them. Used regularly, the strategy increases the students' abilities to form concepts efficiently and also the perspectives from which they can view information."

Bruce Joyce and Marsha Weil, *Models of Teaching*

"Creativity involves breaking out of established patterns in order to look at things in a different way."

Edward De Bono, "The CORT Thinking Program." In *Developing Minds*, A. Costa, editor

"It is good to rub and polish our brain against that of others."

Montaigne

Classroom Story

The teacher has printed on a sheet of paper and run off copies for the number of groups a list of about twenty image-producing words selected from the story about to be read.

TEACHER: "We're going to be reading a story today. In preparation we'll have a look at some of the words you'll meet in the text. Your task is first to tear each word from the sheet your group was given and then to sort the words into five categories. There isn't a right or wrong way to organize these categories. (1) It will be necessary to talk together as you work to put the words into groups. (2)

"One category will be special or unique in some way. It will be up to you to keep the category name a secret from other groups, so you may want to whisper. (3) When you've finished sorting, see if you can predict what the story will be about. I'll be asking one of your group members to tell the class how you sorted the words. We'll hear predictions from the other two members of your group. Are there any questions?"

The teacher had carefully selected groups of three that would be both co-operative and productive. (4) Little time was wasted as working space was set up by each threesome either at a desk or on the floor. Continuous discussion and active participation was immediately evident. They sorted the raggedy-edged words. The vocabulary was challenging and at times debate arose as to the meaning of a word. Before it could be categorized, of course it had to be understood. Careful planning of working groups paid off, on-task time was high, and each group member was busy. Students whispered, huddled together in groups. The teacher circulated, interacting only on invitation.

TEACHER: "Let's come back together now. I was impressed with just how well you listened to one another. Was it sometimes difficult to agree on a category?"

STUDENTS: *"It took us a lot of time to decide on the categories. (5) We told each other why we thought the word went where we put it. When we talked more, it got clearer that words could be sorted in lots of ways."*
"We saw that too. And categories got changed, sometimes to make more words fit."

TEACHER: "I'm glad you remembered what we said at the beginning: there's no right or wrong way. It's important to hear why you think words fit, to hear the associations you made. Let's find out what different groups came up with - Julian, Jefferson, and Erik, would one of you tell us your categories and the other two the prediction?" (6)

STUDENT: *"We had all the deadly things together. Also characteristics of a predator and another category*

Teacher Thoughts

(1) Students make the decisions for categories. Teacher imposing categories limits students' thinking.

(2) Students share prior knowledge and conceptual understanding of the words.

(3) Choosing a unique category stretches students to move beyond the expected response.

(4) Not-yet-able readers are paired with more able.

(5) Learning is enhanced when students reflect on the process.

(6) Sharing thinking deepens understanding of the process.

Teacher Thoughts   **Classroom Story**

with the characteristics of the prey. We put feeling words in another group. That made four categories. The fifth one, the special category, was things to do with the earth, really basic, sun, day and night."

TEACHER: "And your prediction, Erik and Jefferson?"

STUDENT: *"We think it's about an owl. The clues were the talons and it's nocturnal. I think maybe a mouse will be in it because that's what owls prey on."*

She smiled.

STUDENT: *"Night also made us think it was about owls."*

TEACHER: "You've come up with a unique category name, things about the earth, and a prediction you obviously thought about, using the vocabulary you sorted. Is there anything you'd like to tell us about how the process worked for you as a group?"

STUDENT: *"We only got three categories at first. We had to talk a lot about how we could make five, then we got six and that didn't work either. In the end some things just seemed to go together better. We really weren't too sure."*

(7) Valuing the thinker and the thought.

TEACHER: "We sometimes feel anxious when there isn't a clearcut right way. I noticed you struggling with those thoughts. (7) Thank you for sharing.

"Jan, Cameron, and David, who'd like to tell us your categories?"

(8) The open-ended activity allows for meaningful participation of students of all ability levels.

STUDENT : *"We had pretty well the same as the first group. Then we realized that depending on how you looked at the predator and the prey, the list could apply to either. (8) So we put the words together. We also had emotions and an action category like 'swoop' and 'rule' and 'returns.' Our unique category was how things interact with each other and communicate either emotionally or through sound. We put 'kind,' 'listen,' 'heart,' 'sounds,' and 'share' together."*

The teacher inwardly acknowledged the sophistication of their thinking but reacted with a similar low-key and respectful remark to that of the first group. This Grade 6/7 class differed widely in maturity. All listened to the prediction.

TEACHER: "Cameron and David."

Classroom Story   **Teacher Thoughts**

STUDENTS: *"It could be about a proud bird that's a predator. Depending on his moods, he might hunt by day or by night. We thought the prey would be a furry little rodent. The killer would listen in stillness for a heartbeat."*
"You know, the furry little creature would make a pretty decent pet."

The humour is always close to the surface in this accepting atmosphere.

TEACHER: "As you worked together, what were you thinking about?"

STUDENTS: *"It was keener to have to put the words in categories. What I mean is, I knew what all the words meant but I had to think about them in another way to make them fit together. The categories sometimes sort of stretched."*
"Cameron and I wondered where Jan got the words for the unique category 'interact and communicate,' wow!"
"The talking in the group must have done it!"

The class listened to all groups in turn. Each student in each group contributed. (9)

(9) Individual accountability is always recognized in a group effort.

TEACHER: "Now let's read the selection. The vocabulary and predictions have generated lots of ways to work with the same language. Let's see how this author has presented his thinking. The title of the selection is *The Great Gray Owl.*"

Extensions

1. Vocabulary can be chosen from the text and placed on individual cards. The teacher groups the students and gives each group a number of cards to talk about. The cards are processed using the categorizing strategy. ReQuest, Story Grammar, Reading Like a Writer, or simply reading an image and having the students cluster and draft are all ways of leading students to text.

2. Judy Alden had her Grade 1/2 class categorize hawk words that she chose from an article. After the categorizing, she read an image about hawks. The students clustered and drafted. The next day they brainstormed about hawks. The students chose eight favourite facts from the board, wrote them on a fact sheet, drew a picture, and wrote powerful sentences.

Recipe
Sort and Predict

1. Choose twenty image-producing words from a text.

2. Distribute words, one copy to each team of three students.

3. Sort words into five categories, choosing one category that is unique or special.

4. Predict what the story will be about based on the dialogue and student knowledge of the twenty words.

5. Share unique categories and others.

6. In each team, one student reports back on the categories, two on their team's predictions.

7. Reflect on the language circulating around the collaborative thinking.

8. Read the text to confirm predictions.

Story Grammar

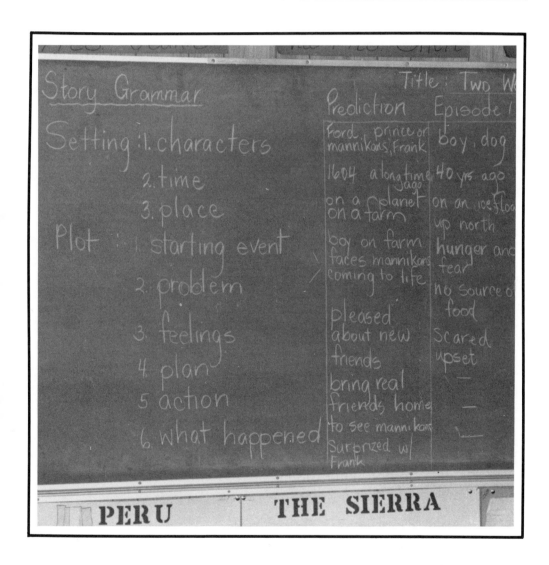

Students of all ages bring to reading a strong sense of story. With this schema as a starting point, and using the Story Grammar Strategy, the teacher leads the students to share their predictions based on story elements. The class reads to confirm its predictions, and predicts again as new information shapes old information. This active participation in the reading process encourages a strong reader/writer dialogue and powerful writing after reading since students gain an understanding of the decisions writers make while composing.

"...learning involves the creation of mental structures. Structuralism involves imagery; children who create images also remember. Once an image is created, it is stored in the brain forever. If a child is creating images while he is reading, he will be learning and also remembering..."

Marjorie Pressley, *The Mind's Eye*

"...capitalize on their collective power...without the help of the group, individual children cannot reach their full potential as writers and readers..."

Donald Graves and Virginia Stuart, *Write From the Start*

"When students have knowledge of the underlying organization of narratives during the process of reading, their reading comprehension is enhanced."

Christine J. Gordon, *Improving Reading Comprehension and Writing: The Story Grammar Approach*

"The most important knowledge is procedural: general procedures of the composing process and specific strategies for the production of discourse and the transformation of data for use in writing. The research indicates that when curriculums begin to focus on such procedural knowledge, they will begin to produce more effective writers."

George Hillocks Jr., *Research on Written Composition*

| Classroom Story | Teacher Thoughts |

Classroom Story

TEACHER: "We're going to be looking at a grid today. It's a kind of chart that will show the different parts of a story. As we work to put what we learn from today's story onto the grid, we'll talk about how a story is organized. We'll see if you find it a useful way to think about the many ideas an author presents in a story. But first, I'm interested in what you already know.

"What is a story?"

STUDENTS: *"Sometimes there are people in it."*
"Yeah, and often they have names."
"Sometimes there are animals that can talk."
"The people can be real or made-up."

TEACHER: "Yes. What else is in a story besides the characters?"

STUDENTS: *"Where it takes place."*
"When it takes place."

TEACHER: "Are there other things in a story we haven't mentioned?"

STUDENTS: *"It has a title."*
"And the title has to go with what the story's about."
"A story can be funny or serious."
"It has to tell what's going to happen."
"It has a very big problem."
"And you have to solve it."
"Yeah, you have to find out who's doing what."
"You have to tell what's going to happen and why."
"You can get ideas from other stories."
"And you tell why you want to write the story."

The Grade 3/4 class has given so many ideas that two chalk boards are filled with their words. The teacher put the Story Grammar grid on the board and together the class and teacher remarked on the features of a story they already knew. The grid was now built up with the already familiar words. (1)

TEACHER: "Look how many ideas you had! You are always amazing me. (2) Now we're going to use the grid to learn about a story."

Teacher Thoughts

(1) It makes sense to the child introducing the structure this way. Imposing the grid without first having them think of what they know about stories can present a formidable form that is just a lot of words and lines. They are now "personally" connected to the items important to a story's organization.

(2) Children tend to be very fluent thinkers when we give them the freedom to fully express their ideas.

Teacher Thoughts

Classroom Story

Framework For Story Grammar   Title: _____

Summary

	Predictions	Episode 1	Episode 2	Episode 3	Episode 4
A. SETTING 1. Characters					
2. Time					
3. Place					
B. PLOT 1. Starter event					
2. Problem					
3. Feelings					
4. Plan					
5. Action					
6. What happened					
C. ENDING					
D. THEME 1. Goal of main character					
2. Intent of author					

TEACHER: "Can you guess its title?"

STUDENT: *"More About Owls."*

Laughs.

TEACHER: "That's a good guess since we talked about owls yesterday."

STUDENT: *"Is it a story about dogs?"*

TEACHER: "Can you guess a title?"

STUDENT: *"The Life of a Dog."*

TEACHER: "That's a title you would like, Cynthia, being such a dog enthusiast. No, the title is different but I think you'll like the story. The title is 'Two Were Left.' What might it be about?"

STUDENTS: *"Birds!"*
"People!"
"Two Boys!"

Classroom Story   **Teacher Thoughts**

"Monsters!"
"Aliens!"
"Santa Claus and Mommy!"
"Me and my Friend!"
"The Principal and the Janitor!"

No shortage of predictions about who the characters might be in H. B. Cave's story, "Two Were Left."

The teacher filled in the grid, taking some of the predictions presented. Having children sitting on the floor in front of the board worked well.

TEACHER: "When might the story take place?"

STUDENTS: "On Saturday."
"Sometime in the dead of winter."
"December 25."
"1999."
"At midnight."
"Spring."
"In the 21st century."

TEACHER: "Lots of interesting ideas for when! What about place? Where might this story happen?"

STUDENTS: "In the jungle."
"On the moon."
"In Vancouver."
"Inside the earth."
"In New York."
"In a castle."
"In Australia."
"In an aeroplane."

TEACHER: "O.K. let's take one idea and see how a story might develop. Angela thought it could be about birds. What might the problem be?" (3)

(3) The students as a group draw on their previous literary knowledge about the interconnectedness of story elements and how a story unfolds. This expectation is key to reading development.

STUDENTS: "It could be about the little birds being left behind when their parents flew south."
"Yes, maybe, 'cause they were too little to fly."
"They could stay together and get strong."
"They could build a nest and have their own babies."

TEACHER: "How do you suppose they felt when their parents left?"

STUDENTS: "Really, really mad."
"Glad."
"Scared."

Teacher Thoughts   **Classroom Story**

"Real glad to be alone."
"Worried."
"No parents to say what to do."
"Terrified."
"Lonely."

TEACHER: "What plan might they make?"

STUDENTS: *"They might practice flying and go south and look for their parents."*
"They could find their old nest where they were laid and wait for their parents to come back."
"They might survive until spring and tell their parents how lonely they were. If they come back..."

(4) The teacher's role is to help students explore possibilities and make connections.

TEACHER: "How do you see the story ending?" (4)

STUDENTS: *"Happy. I like stories to end happy."*
"I like jokes in stories. It could end funny."
"I think they have babies in the spring and their own parents come back and meet their grandchildren. And they tell them how mad they were about them leaving them behind. But it's O.K. now."

TEACHER: "Great. You had lots of ideas about how a story develops. Let's see how H. B. Cave started the story, ' Two Were Left.' I'll read and then stop after a few minutes to hear what you would do with the next stage if you were the author of it."

The teacher read about a third of the story and then stopped. The class discussed the story's setting and plot so far, and the teacher filled the information under the column titled Episode 1.

TEACHER: "What do you predict will happen next? If you were the author, where would you take it?"

STUDENTS: *"I'd have Noni kill Nimuk even though he'd be really, really sorry. But I think it's better if Nimuk dies than Noni. Or both of them. It's the Eskimo way."*
"I'd make the story happy. They'd be found and fed up like it was Christmas dinner."
"I think Noni wouldn't be able to kill Nimuk. The knife is sharp enough but his feelings are too strong. Nimuk isn't just a husky for pulling the sleigh. He's Noni's pet. He's his best friend and a boy couldn't kill his best friend."

Classroom Story

Teacher Thoughts

TEACHER: "Let's see what Noni does."

Teacher read another third or so and stopped.

TEACHER: "What do you see happening?"

STUDENTS: "I see Noni flat on his face in the snow. Nimuk is closing in on him."
"It's tense. I can feel me being Noni, getting ready for Nimuk to bite."

The teacher filled in Episode 2 with the answers students gave.

TEACHER: "Now, as the author, how could you end this story? Or, if you like, how do you predict this author will have this story end?"

STUDENTS: "Well, I'd have them float past a polar bear on another ice floe just before Nimuk could eat Noni. They'd be so glad to have each other's company, they'd hug and then see a fisherman's boat coming toward them. They'd warn him of the polar bear and he'd be so pleased and they'd all share his lunch."
"I think maybe this author will stop Nimuk just in time. He could have him learn to catch fish and Noni could cut them up with the knife he made out of his brace."

After reading to the end of the text, the teacher asked the students to take the role of one of the characters and imagine that they are this character. (5)

(5) By going into role, the student is able to think through the mind of the character.

TEACHER: "Take up your favourite thinking position and relax as I lead you through an image.

Relax...
Close your eyes if you wish...
You are Noni...
Feel the ice raft float...
Feel the cold...
See Nimuk looking at you...
See his eyes...
Hear the creak of the ice...
Feel pain...
Take part of the brace from your leg, hear metal scrape against metal...
See the husky's eyes glow in the darkening light, see the edge taking shape on the knife...

Teacher Thoughts

Classroom Story

It's morning...
The weapon is sharp...
Feel your body turn to steel, the word "Nimuk" form in your throat...
See fear in your dog, hear his breath, the snow crunch, see him dragging slowly, eyes suffering, hungry...
Stand up, sway, fling your tool...
Ouch, you hit the ground...
Hear Nimuk growl, move around your body, above you, hot air against your neck, a scream forms, tongue licking your face, crying, hugging...

---

(6) Students need and want to share their choices. Verbalizing to a partner helps the speaker synthesize and builds belief.

TEACHER: "One, Two, Three, Four, Five. Open your eyes slowly. Turn to the person closest to you. Tell that person what life is like for you as the character you chose."(6)

The children chattered animatedly and the teacher circulated and talked to students who engaged her attention. (7)

(7) The teacher moves toward the students and assumes the role of interviewer. The assumption of role is taken very seriously.

> STUDENT: *"I was so hungry, I could hear and feel the noises of my stomach."*

TEACHER: "You certainly got into role, Angela."

> STUDENT: *"I did, too."*

TEACHER: "What was your life like, John?"

> STUDENT: *"I was real sad killing Nimuk but I had to. I had to live."*

(8) Modelling is critical if the value of writing is to be honoured.

TEACHER: "Now that we've shared your thinking, I'd like you to start to cluster. I'll be working too. (8) If you feel you want to draft before I suggest we start writing, go ahead and get started. Remember to stay in your role from the image. Words about what you see, feel, and think help give a sense of realness to your writing. I'll start the music." (9)

(9) Music creates a serious atmosphere and masks outside noises.

Quiet pervaded the room as children began to cluster. The teacher sat at her desk today, though I had seen her model by doing her writing on the board. A serious, intent mood had taken over from the chatter of moments before. Some students clustered quickly and started on a line they seemed to have already rehearsed! (10) Others were still clustering as the teacher gently pulled the attention toward her.

(10) Individual response time will vary and is respected.

TEACHER: "Just finish the word you're on and begin to play with your cluster. You might like to doodle circles around some words as you think. You might like to link words that go together for any reason in your mind. After a minute or so or whenever you sense something you want to write about, start drafting on every second line."

Classroom Story

Heads were down, everybody clustering, drafting, or musing. Apart from soft piano music, no sounds were heard. After approximately three or four minutes the teacher stopped the writing.

TEACHER: "I know it's hard for some of you to stop writing even for a minute but it really helps some students who are having trouble getting started if they can hear others. Who would like to read their beginning? (11) Jenny."

> STUDENT: *"I'm Nimuk. I'm stranded on an ice floe. There's no piece of meat except Noni."*

TEACHER: "Thanks, Jenny. Would anyone like to respond to Jenny's writing?"

> STUDENT: *"I thought it was a surprise the way it came out that Noni was a piece of meat."*

The teacher chose to have more students share beginnings before directing the class to write for about another seven or eight minutes. (12) Turning the music off she walked around, noticing the lengthy pieces of writing and how most students had written "from the inside."

TEACHER: "You may not have finished but I'd like you to stop now and writer's mumble what you've written so far, listening closely to whether it sounds right. Make any changes that you think would make it closer to sounding right."

A low mumble began as class and teacher read their pieces aloud.

TEACHER: "Did anyone make changes as they read?"

> STUDENT: *"I did. It sounded better to say 'I eyed Noni' than 'I saw Noni.' I said 'saw' lots of times."*

Other changes were noted. Some students elected to write for a few more minutes as the teacher drew to her those either finished or satisfied to leave the draft at that. Sitting on the floor in two concentric semi-circles helped reduce difficulty hearing as some students presented their drafts. After each volunteer, the teacher asked for responses to that piece of writing, focusing the attention on the content, asking for specific words that caused them to see, or feel, or hear, or think what they did. (13) Since no matter was made of who wrote the piece and judgemental words were discouraged, after a while student responses were very specific.

> STUDENT: *"I thought it was funny when you said he came back for fifths, instead of seconds like people usually say."*

Teacher Thoughts

(11) Students who are having difficulty beginning hear the possibilities chosen by other authors. This fuels their thinking without singling out the not-yet-ready writer.

(12) From Donald Graves we have learned the power of the ten-minute write, which we express as "Image—Cluster—Draft."

(13) Through direct questioning, students thought of appropriate responses. The "how" or "why" question brings forth more language.

Teacher Thoughts

Classroom Story

TEACHER: "Is that more effective?"

STUDENT: *"Yeah, it makes me pay attention to it. It's fresher, not ordinary."*

I was deeply impressed with the students' insightful responses to text that I witnessed in this classroom. The teacher-directed lesson would certainly move students to increasing independence in reading comprehension and in written expression. (14)

(14) The combination of shared prediction, imagine, reader/writer dialogue sets the stage for powerful, purposeful, personal expression.

Extensions

Late in September a Grade 1 class read the book *Fireflies* by Julie Brinckloe. They processed the text using the story grammar strategy. The students imaged before drawing and drafting. We were overwhelmed by the depths of understanding shown in the students' writing:

My eyes notice
Some Fire Flies
they Look like
fireworks I blink
And stare at tham they
Fiker And I catch
some And one day I
want to Bed And My
Fire Flies turn what
And green And yellow
tears ran slowly
down my cheek I feel
a smile on My sad face in
My heart I know the fireflies had to be free

one nite I wez
in mie bed room
u got mie windoe I looking
sod Fireflies flieing thin I
rund duoon the stirs
and got a gor thin I
wet uoot to get thin I
thin I Hered my mom Sum Fireflies
colleegni me my mom
thin I wet
in my house
thin I got
my pugamus
on thin got in
my Bed
and wocht the fireflies
thin I sod thim trneeing
green and yellow

DRAFT

This Apichr uv

DRAFT

Firflise
Mdcen Dy2i NS
iN The MOON LiTe
AND The pipL R
CA CHi N The FLiR FLise
TOD

The story grammar structure provided the vehicle for personal expression.

Recipe
Story Grammar

1. With class, brainstorm the grammar of a story.

2. Present the story grammar grid.

3. Collect predictions for the grid, column 1, Predictions.

4. Read the first episode and collect predictions under Episode 1.

5. Continue to read and predict to the end of the text.

6. Read image of story.

7. Each student explains who he or she is in this story to a student partner.

8. Students cluster and write in role.

Anticipation Guide

In a vibrant classroom, learning grows as curriculum as written is bridged to the experiences of the learners. Using the Anticipation Guide strategy, classroom discussion is key. The discussion centres around students' individual responses to teacher-chosen key concepts from text. The teacher orchestrates the voices, but does not share her opinion. Students read to confirm the author's opinion on each of the key concepts. Students write, with increased skill, to defend either their opinions or that of the author. Students thus use the knowledge as presented in the text to expand their world view.

"It is clear that, given the complexity of factors that influence cognitive instruction, strategic teachers do not rely on prepared materials and guides for instruction. They begin as content experts who examine the materials, make decisions about outcomes, and then design instructional activities to match their students' needs for linking to prior knowledge, strategy development, and effective involvement in learning...each author plans for extended sequences of instruction for each of the phases of learning."

Beau Fly Jones, Annemarie Sullivan Palincsar, Donna Sederburg Ogle, and Eileen Glenn Carr, editors, *Strategic Teaching and Learning: Cognitive Instruction in the Content Areas*

"Categories of Teacher Behaviors That Enable Student Thinking Are:

l. Questioning to help students collect and recollect information, process that information into meaningful relationships, and apply those relationships in different or novel situations.
2. Structuring the classroom by arranging for individual, small-group, and total-group interaction; managing the resources of time, energy, space, and materials to facilitate thinking, and legitimizing thinking as a valid objective for students.
3. Responding to help students maintain, extend, and become aware of their thinking.
4. Modeling desirable intellectual behaviors in the day-to-day problems and strategies of the classroom and school."

Arthur L. Costa, "Teacher Behaviors that Enable Student Thinking." In *Developing Minds*

"We cannot treat reading and writing as empty skills, independent of specific knowledge. The reading skill of a person may vary greatly from task to task. The level of literacy exhibited in each task depends on the relevant background information that the person possesses."

E. D. Hirsch Jr., *Cultural Literacy and the Schools*

Classroom Story

TEACHER: "Today's story is using a new strategy called an anticipation guide. What do you think we do when we anticipate?"

STUDENTS: *"Guess?"*
            "Predict?"
            "Get excited?"

TEACHER: "Yes, we look forward to what is going to happen in the story and try and match what we know with what the author tells us.

"I am going to give each of you an anticipation guide. There are five statements on this guide. (1) In the You column, you must put Yes or No (agree or disagree) beside each statement as I read it out. You must make an opinion based on what you think. (2) This is a private time. We will share our thoughts after."

Crossing the Creek
Laura Ingalls Wilder

Directions:
Put Yes or No before each statement under the You column. Be prepared to defend your decisions. After we have read this novel, put Yes or No before each statement, based on the author's opinion. Be prepared to give support from the novel.

You | Author

_____|_____ 1. Horses are strong swimmers.

_____|_____ 2. Long ago, when crossing the prairie, wagons always travelled in groups.

_____|_____ 3. On the prairie, trees mean water.

_____|_____ 4. Starting a campfire on green grass is quite safe.

_____|_____ 5. At night on the prairie it is absolutely silent.

This guide is based on "Crossing the Creek" by Laura Ingalls Wilder, as found in *Ripple Effects*, Nelson Canada, 1983.

The teacher checked to ensure all understood the instructions, then slowly read each statement. (3) "Horses are strong swimmers." She paused for two minutes.

TEACHER: "While you are deciding on whether or not you agree, think of your evidence for your opinion, the reasons why. (4)

Teacher Thoughts

(1) Statements range in number from three to seven. More than seven exceeds student attention.

(2) Individual commitment is necessary on each statement. This begins students organizing their current information.

(3) Teacher reads statements aloud to ensure all can decode the words.

(4) Students are encouraged to elaborate on their opinions. Support from their background experience is necessary.

Teacher Thoughts

Classroom Story

'' 'Long ago when crossing the prairie, wagons always travelled in groups.' ''
She emphasized the "always," reread the statement, but answered no questions. This was individual response time.

Upon completion of the statements, the hush of the room was broken.

TEACHER: "O.K. Pencils down."

(5) Numbers are asked for both yes and no responses. These were recorded to be later validated with the author's opinion.

It was obvious that the students were anticipating the next stage. They were anxious to share their opinions. (5)

TEACHER: "How many said Yes to 'Horses are strong swimmers'?"

20/32

TEACHER: "How many said No?"

12/32

(6) The key to successful learning in this strategy is the classroom discussion.

With each statement she asked for both Yes and No responses. No one was allowed to opt out of a public commitment. She also asked several students on each side to provide support for their opinions. By the fourth statement, hands shot up unsolicited. (6)

TEACHER: '' 'Starting a campfire on green grass is quite safe.' How many said Yes?"

25/32

TEACHER: "No?"

7/32

(7) The students are pulling together their schema and making use of what they know as a prereading strategy.

The students were popping with argument. (7)

STUDENTS: *"Green grass means wet. That's why it's green, so it won't burn."*
"Yeah! That's where you should start campfires. How else can you cook?"
"This is probably long ago, you know, so there's no houses around anyway."
"It's better on grass than in the trees."
"There's no trees on prairies."
"It said trees mean water!"
"Have you ever been there? Did you see trees?"

(8) The teacher does not give a personal opinion. Rather she orchestrates the group talk to allow all voices to be heard.

TEACHER: "I would like to hear from one of the people who said No. Sean? Why did you disagree?" (8)

Classroom Story   **Teacher Thoughts**

      STUDENT: *"I want to change my mind now."*

TEACHER: "Can you remember why you said No?"

      STUDENT: *"Yes, but it's wrong."*

TEACHER: "Why don't you tell us your thinking?"

      STUDENT: *"Well...I just figure that you start campfires in campfire spots like with rocks and stuff."*

TEACHER: "Hmmm - a point worth considering. Anyone else? Julie?"

      STUDENT: *"Well, I saw on TV a huge fire in this open space. And I think they said it burnt under the tall grass part where the other stuff was dry. But I don't know if that's a prairie."*

TEACHER: "Did anyone else see that on TV? Who has more information on what a prairie is?" (9)

(9) The teacher's questions help the students link their experiences to the curriculum content being presented.

She directed the discussion through the fifth statement, then without ever having expressed a personal opinion, unharnessed them into the text.

TEACHER: "In 'Crossing the Creek' by Laura Ingalls Wilder, the author has an opinion on each of these statements. Sometimes she comes right out and says her opinion; sometimes you have to read between the lines to figure it out. When you think you know what she would say to each statement, put Yes or No under the Author column. Be sure to read the whole story. Be thinking of her evidence for her opinion. Don't worry if your opinion differs from hers." (10)

(10) A strong purpose for reading has been set, based on previewed main ideas.

Instantly the readers were open and students were silently reading, searching for confirmation of the major concepts as presented in the Anticipation Guide statements. The bridge between tacit knowledge and explicit knowledge was strong. This was a fine example of personal meaning-making and again, because of all the prereading group talk, no one was hesitating and asking for isolated words to be decoded.

TEACHER: "If you are finished a little early, you might choose to reflect on new information that surprised you. Be sure to collect your evidence carefully."

After all had read the story, discussion resumed.

TEACHER: "How many found the author thought something different than they thought?"

Hands shot up.

Teacher Thoughts

Classroom Story

TEACHER: "The author did surprise you, eh? Did the author also share some of your opinions? Let's see what you think the author's opinion was on each of these statements. 'Horses are strong swimmers.' "

32/32

TEACHER: "Wow! What's your evidence?"

STUDENTS: *"When the family came to that really fast river, the horses swam across pulling the wagons."*
"But the father had to walk in front because the horses were scared."
"And they still went through that really strong current. There was almost rapids."

TEACHER: "OK. So we all agree. Was there enough evidence there to make you change your opinion, or do you think just in this case, the horses were strong swimmers?" (11)

(11) These strategic questions model key learning concepts — i.e., is this a specific example or a generic truth?

The students remained intensely involved in discussion through all five statements. The teacher then switched again to a private, expressive write. (12)

(12) To maintain high levels of learning, students need opportunities for shared thinking and for individual commitment.

TEACHER: "In your journals, I want you to choose one statement that you feel particularly strongly about. Cluster and write for ten minutes. Provide clear evidence for your opinion. Use also the opinions as expressed by the author. You may agree or disagree with the statement and/or the author, but you must give evidence from your experience and from the text. (13) Begin."

(13) Opinion writing involves using evidence from one's experience and from the text for opinion support.

The students clustered, wrote, and finally shared their writing with a partner. The reader read for supporting evidence and starred each new piece. Strong samples were shared. The clarity of thought and elaborate reasoning was incredible. The bell rang and startled me from my musings. An hour and a half had passed!

Extensions

Students may write opinion paragraphs from several of the statements. This provides an opportunity to extend and consolidate their learning as they reconstruct the author's message, melding it with their personal predictions. Use of this guide helps students think critically about what they are reading and relate new information to prior knowledge.

Recipe
Anticipation Guide

1. Identify the major concepts to be learned.

2. Choose concepts that support or challenge children's beliefs.

3. Create three to five simple statements.

4. Keep the statements absolute, personally applicable, generic beliefs rather than merely story-specific.

5. Present the guide *before* reading the text.

6. Students individually *agree* or *disagree* with each statement, as you read them aloud.

7. Poll for numbers of agreement and disagreement on each statement.

8. Students defend their opinions in discussion, providing evidence and example. Teacher does *not* volunteer a personal opinion.

9. Students read silently or in pairs.

10. Students record author's opinion.

11. Discuss similarities and differences in student/author opinion, giving supportive evidence from text and from background knowledge.

12. Cluster and write on one of the major concepts as presented in the statements.

ReQuest

Good readers are active readers who construct meaning as they proceed through text. The ReQuest strategy helps students acquire the strategies of comprehension monitoring through teacher modelling and coaching. The teacher and the class alternate the role of questioner in a group reading. As well as posing and answering questions, the learners model the type of question being asked to heighten the metacognitive awareness of the kinds of thinking involved. On-the-line, between-the-line, and beyond-the-line questions are modelled. Opinion writing as closure for this strategy is rich with supportive evidence from students' experience and from the text.

"Expanding on Bruner's term 'scaffolding', Applebee and Langer (1983) identify five elements 'key to a learning strategy':
1. intentionality - student is motivated to complete a task but needs help
2. appropriateness - task is just beyond student's abilities
3. structure - teacher models and questions using a reasonable framework
4. collaboration - guided neutral feedback is provided to student
5. internalization - student can perform task alone"

Anne Di Pardo and Sarah Warshauer Freedman, *Historical Overview: Groups in the Writing Classroom*

"Manzo, the originator of the ReQuest procedure, suggests...students' abilities to ask their own questions and to set personal purposes for reading...facilitate the students' acquisition of an active, inquiring attitude and their ability to examine alternatives and originate information. These things he considers essential if students are to transfer problem-solving involvement to different contexts."

Robert J. Tierney, John E. Readence and Ernest K. Dishner, *Reading Strategies and Practices: Guide for Improving Instruction*

"...the active use of language processes - composing, comprehending, deliberating, negotiating, is the most effective method for teaching the content of social studies. If the futurists Shane cited are right, focus on such content may be the most effective way to practice and refine these language processes."

Ben Nelms, "Response and Responsibility: Reading, Writing and Social Studies." In *Elementary School Journal*, May 1987

"...students' understanding or misunderstanding of content in literature can be detected in response to "thought questions" that encourage them to state ideas in their own language and to embed their knowledge of basic information in discussions of real issues."

Charles Suhor, "Content and Process in the English Curriculum." In *Content of the Curriculum, 1988 ASCD Yearbook*, Ronald S. Brandt, editor.

Classroom Story

TEACHER: "Today's strategy is called the ReQuest procedure. Does anyone have an idea what it may be about?"

STUDENT: *"Probably predicting. We do lots of that."*

TEACHER: "True. Prediction makes you a more efficient learner. (1) ReQuest involves predicting. ReQuest is an abbreviated word for reciprocal questioning. Any ideas now of what we will do?"

STUDENT: *"Yes. You will ask different kinds of questions.....higher order and harder ones."*

TEACHER: "That's partly true. What about the word reciprocal? What does that have to do with today's strategy?"

One student tried to move into the prefix "re" meaning to repeat, but couldn't seem to explain further than that. The teacher gave some time for the class to team problem-solve, then delivered more information. (2)

TEACHER: "Reciprocal means back and forth. What our strategy means, then, is that as we read a selection on the overhead, we will pause and ask questions. I will ask questions half the time, and you will ask me questions the other half of the time. We will ask three kinds of questions — on the line, between the lines, and beyond the lines. What kind of questions will be on the line?"

STUDENT: *"A question whose answer is found by reading or looking back. It's right there."* (3)

TEACHER: "Right. However, once the story part has been read, I will cover it up so you must be thinking and remembering as you read. (4) The questioner gets to see the selection. However, if you need to reread in order to find an ' on the line ' answer, I'll move my covering paper and allow you to reread.

"What about 'between the lines'? "

STUDENT: *"You read and think more to figure out the answer."*

TEACHER: "True. Sometimes we call those questions inferential because you must use what you know to decide on what the author intended you to believe. Finally, 'beyond the lines' means thinking ahead or predicting or using what you already know from the text and from your experience to anticipate author's intentions.

"OK. Let's begin. The title of our story today is 'The Flowers'. (5) What do you think it is going to be about?"

Immediately the students burst forth with possible themes based on the title of M. Cebulash's story, "The Flowers." They ranged through giving

Teacher Thoughts

(1) Activities in the classroom always have a purpose that can and should be articulated to the students.

(2) Pooled student knowledge is used as a source of information and built on by the teacher.

(3) Students are actively involved in the lesson's directions.

(4) There are no surprises. Students are reminded of all of the teacher's expectations before the task begins.

(5) Always begin ReQuest by predicting from the title to activate student background knowledge and involve them in the learning process.

Teacher Thoughts

(6) This discourages unrelated guessing and webs new information to old.

(7) A wide variety is necessary to discourage a search for the right answer or giving up with merely superficial thinking without exploring alternative possibilities.

(8) Students were chosen based on interest shown during the title predictions.

(9) The rationale behind the activity is explained to the students.

(10) Alternatively, if the print is too small, a reader can read aloud. However, it is preferable that each student read silently. The material should be at an easy reading level while the new comprehension strategy is being introduced.

(11) The teacher articulates strategies of an efficient reader.

(12) Refer back to earlier predictions to link together the experiences and the text.

(13) A question to the entire class involves all students.

Classroom Story

flowers as presents and their functions on other occasions, spring, a story of colours, artists, to a family name Flowers. Each time, she called for clarification and elaboration on the prediction (6) and did not stop until a wide variety of options (7) had been aired. None was given more credence than any other.

TEACHER: "We will read to see how accurate we have been. Since I have already read this story several times, it will be more fun if I have a couple of volunteers join my side for questioning."

Hands flew up. A boy, Jason, and a girl, Susan, were chosen. They moved to stand beside the teacher. (8)

TEACHER: "A review before we go further. We will read this first part silently. Then I will cover it up and Jason, Susan, and I will ask you questions — three kinds of questions, you remember: on the line, between the lines, and beyond the lines. We will tell you what kind of question we are asking. That will help us ask a variety of kinds of questions and help you anticipate our expected response." (9)

The lights in the room dimmed. Eyes were riveted to the print on the overhead. As she recognized that all had read the introduction (an initial paragraph of sixty words), she covered it up and flicked on the lights. (10)

SUSAN: *"Who was sick? On the line question."*
STUDENT: *"That's easy. Gloria was."*

TEACHER: "Often on the line questions are easy, especially when you know a lot about the subject, the text is easy, or you are actively reading and thinking." (11)

JASON: *"Why did the boys want to take flowers to Gloria? Between the lines."*
STUDENT: *"Because the story said that most people liked Gloria and you take flowers sometimes to sick people."*

TEACHER: "All right. Beyond the lines. Were we correct in our predictions about the title?" (12)

STUDENTS: *"It's about giving flowers."*
"It's about graveyards and we said flowers and funerals."
"We didn't predict it would be about stealing."

TEACHER: "We will need to read on to see if the boys do steal the flowers from a grave. Who thinks they will? (13) Let's see. Remember next time you ask we three the questions, so you may want to be thinking of your questions as you read."

Classroom Story

The next section was read silently. The students had responded well to the questioning model. They were eager to ask questions and direct them to any of the three respondents. Most of their questions were between and beyond the lines. They reminded one another to clarify the kind of questions they were asking, and to explain their thinking each time. (14) They were much more particular in justification than most adults I have observed! The teachers occasionally turned a question back on a questioner for his or her opinion. (15)

She allowed approximately ten minutes for the interchange, then continued.

The teacher/student team questioned twice and responded twice. Each section was seventy-five to a hundred words long. At the last stop, the pattern changed. The story states: " 'There's a man outside asking for you,' she (Willie's mother) said. 'He says that you did not pay for the flowers.' "

There was a gasp from the readers as they wondered who this man could have been. The teacher allowed some buzz time, then resumed control.

TEACHER: "Now you must make an assumption — one choice — about who you think this man could be. (16) We are going to brainstorm for possible choices, then vote on which one choice you are prepared to personally defend before we finish reading." (17)

The list ranged from Gloria's father to a ghost to a storekeeper from whom Willie stole the flowers. Once the list had been recorded on the board, each student had one vote for his or her most probable choice.

TEACHER: "Take out your notebooks. In the next ten minutes, you must defend a choice about who you think the man at the door is and prove it to your reader. Mark each piece of evidence you give with an asterisk (*). Your reader will give you a point for each piece of evidence that the reader believes is in support of your choice, whether or not the reader agrees with your choice of man." (18)

The planning took almost two minutes, then students turned to the task at hand. Brows furrowed and the ten minutes passed in a flash. Papers were exchanged, marked according to the established criteria, then returned to the authors. Several fine examples of strong evidence were shared. Every student not only expressed an opinion but could defend it in writing using established criteria. Weak arguments were readily identified. Most impressive was the resounding strength of the students' argument and their task commitment.

The teacher returned to the overhead, flipped it on, and removed the covering paper to reveal the author's choice. A moan escaped. Many students preferred their own choices and began defending their preferences. She prodded with some reflections on the activity.

Teacher Thoughts

(14) Modelling is a very powerful tool for learning. Students want to become Frank Smith's "members of the club" - the club for all people who use written language.

(15) Student/teacher dialogue is enhanced. Knowledge is demonstrably shared, not dispensed by the teacher.

(16) The last break occurs when readers must make a personal commitment. An emotional response with text support makes an easy starting point for opinion writing.

(17) Activities alternate between small groups and total class. Opportunities are always given for individual commitment.

(18) Students need training in opinion/defence writing. Here they have guided practice, with feedback, in posing an argument and defending, with criteria, their position. Further practice occurs in reading another author's defence and recognizing his or her points of evidence even if they are contrary to the reader's own opinion.

Teacher Thoughts

(19) Heightened learning occurs when one reflects on strategies employed and their subsequent effectiveness. Potential refinement for future tasks can occur at this time.

(20) Active involvement at higher levels of thinking over an extended period of time is crucial to enhancing learning.

Classroom Story

TEACHER: "How did the author prepare you? How did he surprise you? Is his choice believable?" (19)

I glanced at my watch. This rapt attention and interest where students had been involved in reading, writing, discussing, and questioning, all at high levels of cognitive activity, had commanded an hour and a half! (20)

Extensions

After the final questions from the teacher, "Is his choice believable?", work from a cluster:

TEACHER: "Take out your notebooks. Put the word 'mud' in the centre of your cluster. Cluster until your brain tells you that you are ready to write, then begin. I will stop you in twenty minutes. You may retell the story, continue it, or react to the author's choices."

Recipe
ReQuest

1. Predict from the title what the class expects the text will be about. Collect a broad range of predictions.

2. Read the first part of the passage together silently. This is usually the first sentence or paragraph.

3. Cover the read passage.

4. The teacher assumes the initial role of questioner. Questions asked are:
   —on the line (literal)
   —between the lines (inferential)
   —beyond the lines (experiential)
   Support for answers can be found by rereading the text, if necessary.

5. The roles of questioner and responder alternate between the teacher and the class.

6. The teacher models good questions and clarifies their type, models good answers, and calls for elaborative thinking.

7. At the final break in the text, predictions are elicited from the students and voted on to encourage personal commitment.

8. Students cluster and write in defence of their choices.

9. Students complete the reading of the text silently.

10. Students confirm and compare predictions with text references.

Matching Thinking

The interrelationships of the reading/writing processes demand that students understand decisions made in the role of reader or of writer - and that students possess a facility for appreciating the thinking of these reciprocal processes. In Matching Thinking, students work in small, mixed-ability, collaborative groups to rearrange a piece of text in an attempt to match the organizational pattern of the author. Students match based on text structure, prior knowledge, stylistic knowledge, and context. This builds a foundation for literary criticism and an awareness of the criteria of sophisticated writing. Retention of the main idea and details of the text is high.

"There is nothing more basic than learning to use one's knowledge in cooperative interaction with other people."

David W. Johnson and Roger T. Johnson, *Cooperation in the Classroom*

"The writer-reader relationship also has been examined from the view of writing and reading as plan-based speech acts. That is, texts are produced by writers who have plans for how they can best communicate with readers; likewise, readers develop plans for making sense out of what writers are trying to communicate."

Donna E. Alvermann, "Integrating Oral and Written Language." In *Research With Reading - Secondary School Reading,* Donna E. Alvermann, David W. Moore, and Mark W. Conley, editors

"The more I delve into children's writing, the more I want to study the connections between reading and writing. The interface between them, I believe, is the research territory of the future."

Lucy McCormick Calkins, *Lessons from a Child on the Teaching and Learning of Writing*

Classroom Story

TEACHER: "Within each of these envelopes I have a puzzle. Your task today is going to be to take the pieces of the puzzle and put them in a form that makes sense. This puzzle makes a newspaper report on someone we know quite a bit about. What are you going to need to think about in order to be efficient in solving this puzzle?" (1)

With this opening in a Grade 5/6 split class, eyes were riveted on the speaker and hands flew up as the students planned their approaches to the posed problem. (2)

> STUDENT: *"I think it's about Rick Hansen."*

Students were able to predict that the article was about Rick Hansen, the Man in Motion, who had just completed his tour around the world in a wheelchair to raise money for spinal chord research.

TEACHER: "How would that help your solving the problem?"

> STUDENT: *"We know lots about him because he's just got to Vancouver."*

TEACHER: "Hmmm...knowing information about what you are going to read would be helpful." (3)

> STUDENT: *"We are going to read all our cards first."*

TEACHER: "Is that effective?"

> STUDENTS: *"Yes! Last time we only read them one at a time and we never all knew the story."*
> *"We're not! We put the cards in three piles and each person organizes her own pile. Then we put the piles together."*
> *"John gives us the cards to read."*

TEACHER: "Each group may want to decide on a plan of attack. There seem to be quite a few choices. Can you change plans midstream?" (4)

Yeas and nays.

> STUDENT: *"We'll find categories like 'blood' in that last one and stick all the blood parts together."* (5)

The enthusiastic sharing continued until the teacher stopped to reorganize the class into groups of three. She stepped quickly through the groups, placing envelopes in front of each group.

TEACHER: "Before you begin, let's reconsider the problem for just a moment."

Teacher Thoughts

(1) Very open-ended directions. No formula is given for solving. The question directs students to examine their available strategies and to pose a tentative plan.

(2) The students are actively involved.

(3) The teacher models reflective thinking re: prior knowledge and its effect on reading comprehension.

(4) Rather than gain group consensus on a plan, she turns back the criteria, "Is that effective?" and reminds each group to choose a plan and that the plan be flexible. This provides training toward independence in learning.

(5) The group sharing of strategies provides an opportunity for students to learn from one another.

Teacher Thoughts

Classroom Story

The students looked as if they could contain themselves for perhaps one minute more.

TEACHER: "This is a newspaper article. What specific story grammar considerations will you need to make?" (6)

(6) Clues are provided focusing on this specific form of text. Students now should access more appropriate textual patterns.

With some prodding, elements such as a strong opening with lots of detail, the five newspaper questions (Who? What? When? Where? Why?), and a great title were given.

TEACHER: "Okay. Remember your plan and the fact that this is a newspaper story. You have fifteen minutes. Begin."

(7) Collecting samples of student talk allows her to build the remainder of this lesson and the next from the experiences of the students; linking "curriculum as lived" with "curriculum as written."

The flurry of activity was incredible! Almost spontaneously, triads of students poured over their cut-up stories, engrossed in the thinking of trying to retell the story as the author. The teacher smiled smugly, a magician reborn, as she wandered inconspicuously among the groups, listening to and incidentally recording the students' talk. (7) She called a time out after ten minutes.

TEACHER: "I have a question. Considering that this article is from a newspaper, there may be an especially important consideration for the beginning." (8)

(8) Teacher intervention and refocusing of direction based on student response to text. The direction is built from shared student responses.

STUDENT: *"We knew this was Rick Hansen."*

TEACHER: " Yes. Lucky prediction. Can you tell what I was reading on the week-end?"

STUDENTS: *"Yeah!"*

TEACHER: "Have you chosen a beginning? Have you discovered some criteria for a beginning?" (9)

(9) Good decision-making involves establishing criteria.

STUDENTS: *"It should say his whole name and not Rick or he. Or you don't know who you are reading about."*

TEACHER: "Hmmm...how many groups thought of that?"

STUDENTS: *"It's got to start with lots of information. Like a newspaper doesn't begin 'Once upon a time...'"*
"But it could start with him as a baby."

Nods.

STUDENT: *"Nope. That just says Rick."*

Classroom Story

TEACHER: "Sometimes it's wise to organize a beginning and pull in your clues from there. Think carefully as a group and make a wise decision. (10) Remember how language can be hooks for linking. I'll give you ten more minutes. This is a hard one." (11)

The group experienced success and frustation as they struggled to reach consensus and reconstruct the article. All were involved. All were reading. All were actively problem-solving, in interdependent groups.

All too soon, the twenty minutes was up. Most groups had achieved a completed draft. Before reading the author's version, they brainstormed as a total class, "What made our group work well?"

The original article was distributed. Moans of despair and squeals of delight burst forth. Again the teacher wrestled control and directed student thinking.

TEACHER: "How closely did you come to the original version? Are both versions acceptable? Are there many patterns for presenting the same truth? Whose version do you prefer? Yours? The reporter's? Why?

"Let's examine some specific choices the author made. What thinking would he have been doing as he wrote? Did he achieve his purpose? What thinking were you doing as you made choices as a reading writer? Did yours flow?" (12)

Forty-five minutes had passed, but still she pressed on, pushing at the limits of the students' critical thought; examining, questioning, reflecting, congratulating. (13) Every student was caught. They recognized the magnetism of the moment and the inherent power in mastering control of the process.

TEACHER:"Let's talk briefly about choices again. Your selection may be quite different from the author's, but yours still may work. Readers and writers have many choices to make as they create. Your choice may be good without being the same choice as the author's.

"In your logs, take five minutes and reflect on these two questions: (14)
    l. What made my group work well? (15)
    2. What would I do differently next time?" (16)

Again, pens flew across papers, thoughts concentrated, a pause, then writing again.

TEACHER: "Anyone have a special thought to share? Did you enjoy that? I am really impressed with how hard you worked!" (17)

Teacher Thoughts

(10) Not are you right or wrong, but how many considered this information to be important and relevant? Students are continually coached into refining their existing knowledge and putting this knowledge to work for them.

(11) Extends the time allotment to ease student frustation.

(12) There is no exclusive right answer. An examination is made of choices - readers' choices and writers' choices and the thinking behind them.

(13) Students can and should be engaged in meaningful, sustained activity for extended periods of time.

(14) An individual log provides an opportunity for individual reflection and commitment.

(15) Focus on the process before the product.

(16) Students examine their strategies and hypothesize changes for the next time. Teacher provides external evaluation.

(17) Recognition of the effort and the joy of learning.

Extensions

1. As follow-up to the Matching Thinking Strategy the following day, students returned to their cooperative groups and clustered the content that they remembered from the newspaper article. A sample generated in fifteen to twenty minutes of group work time is included.

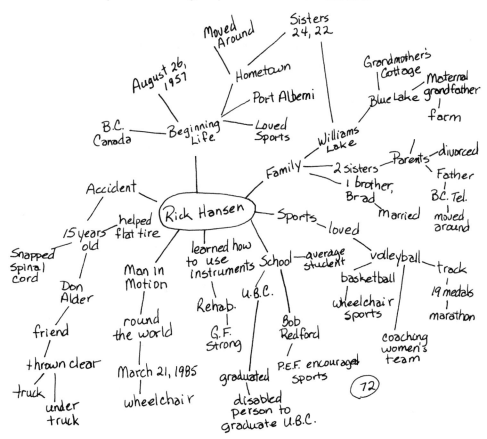

2. This strategy focuses attention on both content and form. The way form controls language choice and language structure becomes apparent to the students. They gain an appreciation of reaching for language within structure.

3. Learning logs are very helpful in teaching self-analysis and documenting growth in metacognitive processes.

4. As students engage in small group work, teachers collect comments made by students that reflect their thinking. These serve as strategic models for students and as documentary evidence of metacognitive growth. Samples collected in the scripted class follow.

> "Most times you have to think about beginning/middle/end. This time you had to think about the last time you read a newspaper. Boy, what a difference!"
> "Finding a place to begin was really hard!"
> "We thought about one piece really carefully, then found what hooked on after."
> "Next time we put all our pieces on the table to read."
> "I'm better at this because of being a storyteller."

Recipe
Matching Thinking

1. Choose an article or a story for the students to reconstruct.

2. Cut an article into segments and place in an envelope.

3. Assign students to cooperative groups of three.

4. Review, as a class, strategies that help in hooking story segments to one another.

5. Allow twenty minutes for student teams to organize the segments into a cohesive article.

6. Brainstorm, as a class, "What made our group work well?"

7. Compare student articles with author's version.

8. Share strategies used by the teams during the problem-solving process.

9. Compare students' decisions with authors' decisions.

10. Write in log books, reflecting on the process.

Chapter 10

Metaphor

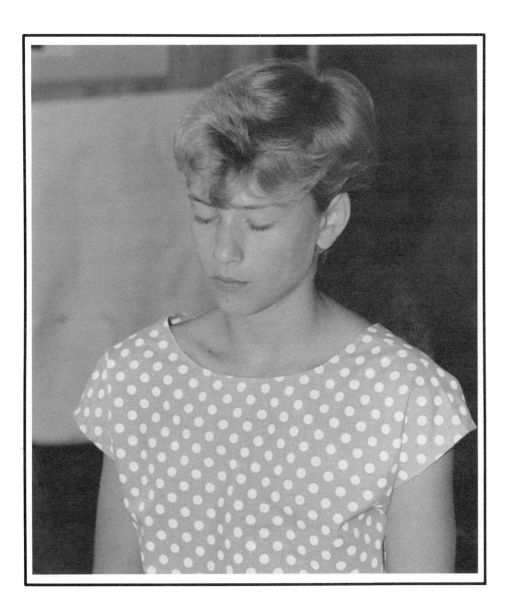

The Metaphor Strategy is a sophisticated play with language. As a whole class, as early as Grade 2, students analyze metaphors and write their own. Steps in the strategy include imagery, attribute listing, and the use of Venn diagrams. The strategy helps make the unknown known, building from personal experience and imagination.

"Metaphor is a tool that relates content to prior experience and knowledge in a creative diagnostic way that
calls for imaginative, critical analysis."

John Barell, Presentation at Pre-Conference Institute,
ASCD Convention. San Francisco, CA, April 1985

"Analogies and metaphors are the threads by which the
mind holds onto the world...Moreover, in the thinking
process, they serve as models to give us our bearings...
(Arendt, 1977)"

David N. Perkins, *The Minds Best Work*

"Metaphors can be a bridge for creative insight, connecting what your students already know to what you want
them to know."

Donald A. Sanders and Judith A. Sanders, "Capturing the
Magic of Metaphor." In *Learning 87*, February

"Stories are a way of making sense - of giving meaning to
obvservable events by making connections between
them."

Gordon Wells, *The Meaning Makers*

Classroom Story

        Diamonds, diamonds, and more diamonds
        Twinkling, shimmering, sparkling
        In the sand
        Here,
        There,
        And as far as I could see

This poem, written by the teacher, was read several times together by the Grade 3/4 class.

TEACHER: "Why do you think I like this poem?"

    STUDENTS: *"Because it's on the beach."*
                    "Because it makes a picture."

TEACHER: "Let's think about that picture for a moment. Close your eyes while I read the poem again. See what pictures come to your mind. We will share them in a few minutes." (1)

Eyes closed and the teacher quietly and slowly reread the poem. She gave an additional moment's pause.

TEACHER: "Open your eyes. Who had a strong image or picture?"

    STUDENTS: *"I was at my grandma's cottage in the summer.*
                    She's got a really great beach with lots of sand
                    and no rocks."
                    "Yeah. Me too."
                    "I felt hot in the sun."
                    "Mm!"
                    "I saw the desert. There's sand there too."

TEACHER: "What words did the poet use to help you draw these strong pictures so quickly?" (2)

She underlined the adjectives "twinkling, shimmering, sparkling" as they were given but stopped with "sand" and "diamond" and rewrote them separately on the board.

TEACHER: "Let's talk about the diamonds. How many of you people have been to a sandy beach on a sunny day? How many have seen sunny sandy beaches on TV? Did you see any diamonds there?" (3)

    STUDENTS: *"No"* - and grins.

TEACHER: "Why did this poet say he saw them?"

    STUDENTS: *"He didn't. The sand looks like that in the sun*
                    because parts of it sparkle."

Teacher Thoughts

(1) Visual thinking is integrated into the reading to deepen the personal images of the readers/listeners. Students connect their personal experiences with the author's text.

(2) Specific attention to diction used in image creation. Skills teaching is from within the context of an integrated, meaningful whole.

(3) Building the metaphor from personal experience of the students.

Teacher Thoughts

Classroom Story

"Yeah. It reflects the light."
"And sometimes pieces of sand hurt when you step on them and that could be diamonds too."

(4) An early form of attribute listing, a skill necessary for creating and enjoying metaphoric language.

TEACHER: "If I had never seen or heard of a diamond, how would you show it to me?" (4)

STUDENTS: *"It sparkles."*
"It's sort of white."
"It's rich."
"It means you have a husband."
"It's hard."
"It's a ring."
"My mom has earrings too."
"It can scratch glass. I heard that."

TEACHER: "That's very good. Can you see how this poet, when he called the sand diamonds, helped us make connections? Our brains think of all the things we know about diamonds and the poet helps us think those same things about the sand in the sun that he's telling us about. This gives us a better picture and makes us look at sand in a new, more imaginative way. Also, in case we have never seen sand sparkle in the sun, he helps us picture what it looks like by describing it in a way with which we are familiar - the way diamonds sparkle. (5)

(5) Teacher explains the rationale of metaphors, the how-to and the why. Students need knowledge of the skill and knowledge of when to use it.

"This tool is called a metaphor. It's very sophisticated. It helps us explain unfamiliar things by comparing them to familiar things, things we know about. When we write it also helps us present ideas to our readers in interesting ways. Let's try one." (6)

(6) Building from a model using shared expertise of the group.

She began by putting "story" on the board, then brainstormed with the class for all the characteristics of a story or parts that make up a story. Twenty to thirty phrases and words were given. This was repeated with "seeds." (7)

(7) Individual attribute listing. Comparisons are not made at this point.

TEACHER: "Reflect on what we have done, and think for a moment of ways that stories and seeds are similar. We will have three minutes of think time before I hear any ideas." (8)

(8) More complex responses are given as a result of wait/think time. This deepens the level of response and understanding.

The class responded although several were anxious to share immediately. I wondered whether cognitively the students would grasp the abstract task demanded. I was soon to be taken quite aback with their sophistication.

STUDENTS: *"When you begin to write a story, it's like a seed growing in your mind."*
"The end of a book is the flower wilting."
"Seeds have covers to protect them. So do books."

Classroom Story

"Roots are characters that hold the story together."

TEACHER: "Wow! I am constantly amazed at how well you can think! Let's join some of these words into one shared category. The rule for coming into this category is that they describe stories and seeds. This will help us find more comparisons." (9)

A Venn diagram was used to help present a stronger visual impact of shared characteristics (attributes). The students, as a group, discovered that not all their descriptors were common to both.

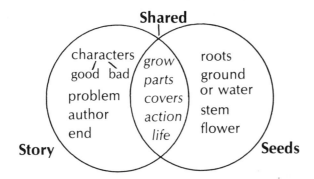

TEACHER: "Our final activity on metaphors is writing. We began this morning with you reading like a writer to understand the author's picture of sand. Now I want you to try and write for a reader who you want to understand that stories are like seeds in some ways. (10) This is really hard. (11) You will need to think lots and probably write little. Try to make your reader understand what a story is by showing him or her through seed descriptions. Think hard. Let your mind wrestle with the problem."

The class settled into the challenge. Some began with a cluster, others had had enough preparation and began writing. This "show me with words," with the students being aware of their reasoning, had lasted for more than an hour. (12)

Student Samples

now a seed is like a story well a seed grows when you water it and a story grows when you think about it it is like watering a plant Only you thing about it that is all have to do.
    Jane, Grade 2

Teacher Thoughts

(9) Shared traits provide more support for those still struggling after some students have made initial connections.

(10) Reading and writing are constantly taught as reciprocal thinking processes.

(11) This is a very complex task. Mastery is difficult. The level of difficulty should be acknowledged.

(12) With more sophisticated or practiced learners, discourage the use of similes: comparisons that use like or as. The refinement of using metaphors, not similes, occurs with guided practice.

DRAFT

The story has an adventure in it. The seed does too. Wind blows the seed away and goes somewhere else and grows and needs adventure. Storyies grow when the author has more thought and its a adventure.
  Christine, Grade 3

DRAFT

The story began in spring when the seeds were planted. The story grew and grew until it ended. Millions and millions of tiny seeds growing and growing until the plant died. With seeds you learn and with story you can learn too. Seeds with shells, books with covers. Inside a seed shell there is a seed and inside a book there are words. Seeds have colour and so do stories. Some seeds are soft and some books are soft too. Seeds need to be took care of. Seeds need sunlight, water, soil, heat and air to grow. Books need to be took care of too. You should not scratch rip or wright on the book.
  Jeffrey, Grade 4

DRAFT

A writers thoughts are at first small
But then it grows, sprouts and branches to different ideas and topics.
He doesn't keep his thoughts fenced up
But he opens the gate and sets them free from the weeds
Then plant and make his thoughts grow again.
  Kelly, Grade 6

Recipe
Metaphor

1. As a class, read and analyze a metaphor.

2. Discuss what metaphor is and how it connects for us.

3. Choose two words to be compared.

4. List attributes of each of the words.

5. Orally share metaphors based on attribute listings.

6. Using a Venn diagram, categorize shared attributes.

7. Cluster and write own metaphor.

8. Discuss the success of the implied comparisons.

Reading Like a Writer

The use of the Thinking Paper in the Reading Like a Writer Strategy has created a great deal of fun in elementary classrooms. Students quickly capture the drama of a story unfolding around them, the magic every good reader knows of being wrapped within a story. As the teacher reads, the students write their predictions of what will happen next or of what decision they would make if they were the author. These thoughts are shared with partners and the class before the story continues. Meaning making is thus a natural process. The ensuing thoughtfulness is reflected in students' personal writing.

"...the reader uses information to form hypotheses or predictions about the meaning of the text and the author's intentions. The hypotheses and predictions thus become the purpose for reading...the reader reads in order to confirm or reject them..."

Beau Fly Jones, Annemarie Sullivan Palincsar, Donna Sederburg Ogle, and Eileen Glenn Carr, editors, *Strategic Teaching and Learning: Cognitive Instruction in the Content Areas*

"...instructional procedures that introduce strategies as they are needed in the context of actually understanding texts, where the strategies are demonstrated over time, and where the student is fully informed of the purpose of the strategy, produce long-lasting, significant improvements in reading comprehension scores."

Ann L. Brown, *Teaching Students to Think as They Read: Implications for Curriculum Reform*

"Curiosity and prediction go hand in hand. They are the mainstays of prereading instruction. The more students predict as they read, the more they will read with certainty and confidence; the greater their curiosity, the greater their motivation to read."

Richard T. Vacca, *Content Area Reading*

"...reading is an event in which thoughtful readers act as composers...no one can be a thoughtful reader unless and until one reads as if one were a master writer..."

P. David Pearson and Robert J. Tierney, *On Becoming a Thoughtful Reader: Learning to Read Like a Writer*

"Authors also show children how to write. How else than by reading, or being read to, could children, or anyone else, learn all the subtle conventions of plot, narrative, characterization, mood, style - or of spelling and punctuation for that matter? You have to read in a special way to learn about writing in this manner, you have to read like a writer, like a member of a club."

Frank Smith, *Insult to Intelligence*

Classroom Story

TEACHER: "Today we are going to read like writers. How do you think writers read?" (1)

STUDENTS: *"They invent as they get into a story."*
"I think questions come into their heads as they read."
"I think they guess what will happen and they feel good if it turns out to be true."
"I think they read to get new ideas for their own stories." (2)

TEACHER: "In this strategy we will be using a thinking paper. I will read the story to you in four parts. After each part we will share what the author's words made us think about. Then you will write down what you think will happen next. We know that successful readers do a great deal of predicting. (3) To begin, take your thinking paper and fold it into four just like the model on the blackboard. Number the spaces."

Thinking Paper
1.
2.
3.
4.

Before reading from Mem Fox's story, "Swans and Peacocks," the teacher invited students to predict from the title.

TEACHER: "The title of the story is ' Swans and Peacocks.' What do you think it will be about?" (4)

The Grade 3/4 students pondered thoughtfully.

STUDENTS: *"Life in a pond."*
"How swans and peacocks live."
"An adventure with lots of animals."
"Swans and peacocks on a farm."

The teacher read the first few paragraphs.

TEACHER: "What were you thinking about as I read the words?" (5)

STUDENTS: *"I see beautiful peacocks getting upset."*
"I was thinking about peacocks huddled together listening to one peacock speak."
"I saw a castle falling down and birds in the garden."

Teacher Thoughts

(1) This beginning activates schema and taps procedural knowledge.

(2) The context for the reader-writer dialogue is established.

(3) Teacher explains procedures they will use and their rationale.

(4) Begin to activate schema with title predictions.

(5) Imagery development prior to reading increases comprehension.

Teacher Thoughts

Classroom Story

The teacher read another paragraph and then asked another question.

(6) Students are building meaning from the cues provided by the story.

TEACHER: "If you were the writer, what would you make happen next? Write your thoughts down in the first space on your thinking paper. (6)

(7) Valuing individual thought sets the stage for a risk-free environment.

"Your thinking might be different from the author's thinking. You cannot be wrong in your thinking." (7)

She paused while the students wrote.

TEACHER: "Turn to the person beside you and share your thinking. If you haven't written something yet, share what you were going to write. (8)

(8) Networking thoughts through active participation.

"Who would like to share their thinking with the class? What do you think will happen next?"

STUDENTS: *"They will find a way to get rid of the swans."*
"Peacocks have a meeting and decide to go talk to the swans."
"They work continuously for many days to put up a wall between the lake and the garden. It grew and grew."
"Spy on the swans and start a fight."
"The peacocks will brag about how beautiful they are."
"I think the peacocks will start to fight with the swans." (9)

(9) Total group sharing helps students formulate hypotheses and identify with the characters and setting.

The teacher read the next episode.

TEACHER: "What are you thinking about now?"

STUDENTS: *"War."*
"Birds getting worked up over nothing."
"I see two flocks of birds fearing each other."
"I see the birds preparing to protect themselves." (10)

(10) The author-reader connection is continued and strengthened as meanings are redefined.

TEACHER: "If you were the writer, what would you make happen next?"

The students eagerly wrote their thoughts as they engaged with the conflict. When most of the students had completed their projections, the teacher invited them to share their writing with the person next to them. (11)

(11) This technique allows every voice to be heard.

TEACHER: "Does anyone want to share their ideas with the class?"

A sea of hands went up.

Classroom Story   **Teacher Thoughts**

STUDENTS: *"They will have a fight and see who wins."*
"The swans make more arrows."
"The peacocks will be outnumbered, but soon they will be quiet."
"The swans and the peacocks will get to be so terrified that they both will go and make new homes somewhere where nobody will ever know any others but themselves."
"The peacocks are not going to fight." (12)

(12) The students are crafting their understanding.

The teacher continued reading the text. Every student listened expectantly. The pencils began writing before the teacher posed her challenge.

TEACHER: "If you were the writer, how would you end this story?"

Once again the students wrote, then shared their ideas with a partner. (13) Many hands waved excitedly indicating students wanted the whole group to hear their speculations on the conclusion.

(13) Predictions are now based on literary knowledge and experience with this text.

STUDENT: *"An egg that had not been hatched just did and birds started all over."*

TEACHER: "How did you reach this conclusion?"

STUDENTS: *"Well, the writer wiped out all of the birds. I knew there must have been some eggs, so life would continue."*
"They get annoyed."
"They become friends."
"They should stop fighting and never see or talk to each other again."
"A small peep sounded through the silence of the gardens and the lake. A small fragile baby swan waddled out into the quiet."

TEACHER: "How did you decide on your ending?"

STUDENT: *"I did the same as Margo. I knew there had to be eggs."*

TEACHER: "Thank you for sharing your thoughts. When we share our thinking, we all get new ideas. Let's hear how Mem Fox ended her story." (14)

(14) Acknowledging and respecting all contributions is common.

The teacher read the conclusion. Some eyes sparkled as their thinking matched the author's. Others quickly revised to bring their thinking in line with the author's thinking.

The teacher stepped closer to the class.

Teacher Thoughts

(15) The image facilitates deep processing to expand thinking.

(16) Further processing helps the student internalize meaning.

(17) This oral rehearsal is preparation for writing.

(18) Role-playing helps students identify with elements of the text while the dialogue builds belief.

Classroom Story

TEACHER: "I'm going to read some words to you now that will help you get inside the story. (15) Put yourself in a comfortable thinking position."

> See yourself in the gardens...
> Notice the peacocks...
> Hear the making of plans...
> Notice the swans tremble...
> Feel the night air tense...
> Hear the silence...
> Notice the eggs...
> See the hatching...

TEACHER: "You've created a picture in your mind of what life was like for the swans and peacocks. I want you to stay with that picture for a few minutes. Talk to yourself in your mind about what you are seeing...feeling...hearing...noticing..."(16)

The teacher waited until one student had stirred.

TEACHER: "Turn to the person beside you and share what life was like for the swans and peacocks." (17)

The students talked with great enthusiasm. She stopped them after two to three minutes of discussion, then moved into the class in the role of a traveller.

TEACHER: "I've just come into the gardens. I notice some fighting going on. Could you tell me what is happening here?" (18)

STUDENT: *"The swans and peacocks are fighting."*

TEACHER: "Who are you?"

STUDENT: *"I'm a peacock and I'm afraid."*

TEACHER: "Is there another peacock here? What is life like for you?"

STUDENT: *"Well, we got pushed into a fight. I'm sharpening arrows. Those swans might get us."*

TEACHER: "I see. Is there anyone else here who can help me understand what is happening?"

STUDENTS: *"I'm a mouse in the kingdom and I'm very scared. Arrows are crashing very near my nest." "I'm a wise old owl peeking through the branches. Those silly birds think they are enemies. I'll have to settle this once and for all."*

Classroom Story   **_Teacher Thoughts_**

TEACHER: "How will you stop the fight?"

The students pondered.

TEACHER: "Does anyone have some advice?"

STUDENTS: _"He could fly over to each side and tell them to
be friends."
"He could call a meeting for everyone in the
kingdom."_

TEACHER: "Put your hand up if you know who you are in the kingdom.
Write down who you are in space number 4...now turn your thinking
paper over. Put a circle in the middle of the page. Put who you are in
the middle of the circle. Begin your cluster showing what life is like for
you in this story."

The teacher began her cluster of her character on the board. (19) After   (19) Modelling shows the
three to four minutes she stopped the students.   valuing of writing.

TEACHER: "Circle your most powerful words. Draw lines to words that
connect. When you are ready, begin writing on the new paper that I will
bring around. Show what life is like for you in the kingdom."

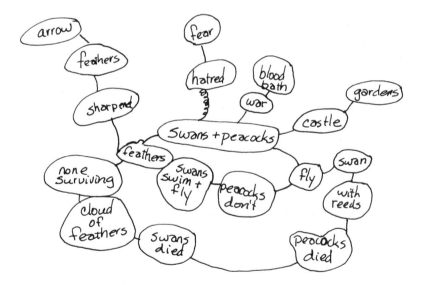

The teacher passed out new papers, then began drafting on the board.   (20) Anyone talking is asked
After four to five minutes she stopped the class. (20)   to talk inside his or her head.
                                                                                Quiet encourages the expres-
                                                                                sion of thought.

TEACHER: "Read out loud what you have written so far. (21) Would
anyone like to share a beginning?"   (21) The writer's mumble
                                                                               helps the student hear the
                                                                               meaning being expressed.

Teacher Thoughts

Classroom Story

I swim in the glisning water of blue lake Quietly listening to the under water noises. I hear faint crys from above I gently swim to the waters edge. feathers peacefully fly up in the meaningful sky making clouds. Blood shoots in puddles. Everything is Mournfully Quiet. It is over!
Cory

TEACHER: "Continue writing. When your writing feels finished, read it over to yourself. Hear if that is really what you want to say. Feel free to make any changes. Cross out what you don't want. Add new words where they feel right."

After five to six minutes, or when a few writers seemed finished, the teacher invited the students to do a further writer's mumble. (22)

(22) Students distance themselves to match what is actually written with their thinking.

TEACHER: "Read your writing to yourself. Writers do this all the time to see if their writing makes sense and sounds right.

"We are going to begin sharing now. When you feel finished, please join us on the carpet."

The sharing began with Cory slipping into the writer's chair. After he presented his draft, the class applauded and he chose the next presenter. Only volunteers were heard from.

TEACHER: "We've certainly heard some powerful language today. I think Mem Fox would be very pleased to hear these pieces of writing.

(23) Often young readers and writers are deeply touched by fine literature.

STUDENTS: *"Maybe we could send her a book of the thoughts we wrote after hearing her story." "I wonder what other stories she's written." (23)*

(24) Class reviews the strategy and reflects on the process.

TEACHER: "What did we do today?" (24)

STUDENTS: *"We read a story and guessed what would happen next." "We were thinking like writers as we heard the story."*

(25) The reflection equips the students with a new tool for processing print.

TEACHER: "Why do you think we used this strategy today?" (25)

STUDENTS: *"Well, it helped us to think of ways a story could go. It was kind of like a river going this way and that." "It gave me a new way to read my library book. I think it's fun to think like a writer because I am a writer."*

Extensions

Concept Mapping

1. The next day the teacher might have the students brainstorm key ideas from the story in small, mixed-ability groups. The groups make a list of words that helped create a picture of that story.

   After five minutes of student collaboration, the teacher invites them to share their lists. She then puts six or eight circles on the blackboard (leaving spaces between the circles).

   TEACHER: "Look at your lists and give me a word or phrase to put in each circle."

   TEACHER: "Look at the words. I wonder how we could connect the ideas."

   STUDENTS: *"You could connect fear and gardens because a cloud of fear surrounded the gardens."*
   "You could connect those words another way. The animals were hiding because they felt frightened in the gardens."

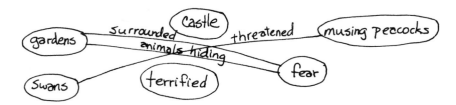

   To deepen student connections with the story, give each student a sheet with six circles on it and have them build their own concept maps. They may add more circles. Further questions that the students generate move them to a new stage of fact gathering.
   Thanks to Intermediate Helping Teacher Sheila Borman for her help with this extension.

2. With young children the teacher might cut up the story's sequence and give it in an envelope to a small group to reconstruct. Once the students put the story together, they could prepare a dramatic retelling. When many stories have been internalized, the teacher could give out a different story to each group of three. The groups would act out the story for the others to guess the title.

3. One experiment we did with the swan and peacock story was to process it using Reading Like a Writer in a Grade 2 class. We left the story for a

month; then the teacher stepped in one morning with the words:
"I'm hearing some unusual sounds in the gardens today. Who can tell me what is happening near the castle today?"

A student replied:
"Those peacocks are up to no good again."

Soon all of the students were in role, recalling the story. We followed Stuart from initial predictions to cluster to draft, and then to his second draft and published piece one month later.

Thinking Paper
1. They will find a way to get rid of the swans.
2. The peacocks are not going to fight.
3. They are going to mate.
4. I was a frog in the moat.

Predicting as the story is being processed

I am a frog   Stuart
At first I heard the voice of a peacock. Then I heard shrill cries. When I hopped closer, I saw blood-stained land. And blood tattered birds. Each with an arrow through it's body. They were all dead. Then I saw more birds fighting. So I screamed, "Stop stop why must you fight? You will kill everyone of you and you will become extinct from this land. Stop I say". And the leader said "You are right we will go in peace" So they laid down their weapon and walked away.

First Draft

Cluster and draft,
one month later.

There was a sudden
silence ~~silence~~ that
surrounded the garden and
the murky waters of the
blood filled pond. A touch
of sadness was floating
to my heart. There was a
tote of sorrow in my voice.
And suddenly there were
war cries and the number
of arrows was more and
more. I couldn't beleive it.
More and more birds died.
More and more arrows flew.
I bounded through it all
scattering birds this way
and that. Still it did not work.
I was not a match for them.
I shouted, "Those . . . .

There was a silence that surrounded the garden and the murky water of the blood filled pond. A touch of sadness was floating to my heart. There was a note of sorrow in my voice. And suddenly there were war cries and the number of arrows was more and more. I couldn't believe it. More and more birds died. More and more arrows flew. I bounded through it all and shouted. "Those arrows are no sharper than my antlers. Why must you fight? WHY?" But they did not stop.

Published piece

Stuart

Recipe
Reading Like a Writer

1. Distribute "thinking papers" to students.

2. Predict, as a class, from the title.

3. Read aloud to class, stopping three times with questions such as "If you were the writer, what would you have happen next?"

4. With each question, students write on their papers in the appropriate box, share with one another, and with the class as a whole.

5. Read image of story.

6. Students assume role of character and write this in the fourth box.

7. Interview students in role.

8. Have students cluster and draft what life is like for them in the role of the character they chose from the story.

Chapter 12

On to Publishing

Teachers strive to improve students' thinking. Teachers also strive to improve the quality of student published work - work that accurately reflects the high standards of student thinking and student knowledge of the conventions of print. This chapter discusses several means of drafting thought within form and discusses strategies for successful Writers' Workshop. Central to fine student writing, however, is a heavy emphasis on pre-writing and pre-reading. This eases the burden of editing and proofreading and enables students to focus on becoming thoughtful, reflective learners, empowered with strategies for refining their craft.

"The focus of instruction with the greatest power is...inquiry...(It) involves using sets of data in a structure...to help students learn strategies for using data in their writing."

George Hillocks Jr., *Research on Written Composition*

"The greatest barrier to writing and spelling development is the excessive emphasis given to standard spelling...what matters during initial composing is that children develop spelling strategies which enable them to write with a degree of fluency."

Wendy Bean and Chrystine Bouffler, *SPELL by Writing*

"...only through reflection the writer is involved as a learner."

Bernard D. Harrison, "The Pleasure of Writing." In *The Writing of Writing*, Andrew Wilkinson, editor

"...in a writing conference...not only does the teacher reflect what is in the writing, but she also encourages the student to reflect on the experience itself - to talk about the experience itself. So the writer can achieve a double kind of distance - distance on the text and distance on the experience depicted in a text...the groundwork for expansion is laid."

Susan Sowers, "Reflect, Expand, Select: Three Responses in the Writing Conference." In *Understanding Writing K-8*

"Computers may not take care of every aspect of writing, but they can do a great deal to help all kinds of people to see themselves as writers and to perform more like professionals."

Frank Smith, *Insult to Intelligence*

"...the concern for use of standard spelling should not be permitted to interfere with the creative process of composing. Checking and correcting spelling can be considered as part of proofreading and editing."

Kenneth S. Goodman, E. Brooks Smith, and Robert Meredith, *Language and Thinking in School*

Classroom Story

Purpose drives the whole process. When the teacher moves into editing, her students have spent time shaping their thinking. If they were studying owls, they may have many clusters and drafts recorded in their personal learning logs or reflective journals. In the first phases of the Reading-Writing Cycle they were writing to learn. Now that their learning has been refined, the teacher decides to have that thinking moulded into a finished piece. Depending on her purpose, she will decide an appropriate form to use.

Writers' Workshop

TEACHER: "We've been working very hard on our owl study. You have written many drafts. Now we are ready to publish what we've learned. I wonder what shape would work best for the knowledge we have." (1)

STUDENTS: *"We could write magazine articles."*
"We could write owl poems."
"We could write letters to friends showing how much we know."
"We could write a TV documentary." (2)

TEACHER: "How could we turn what we know into a magazine article? We haven't used that form yet."

STUDENTS: *"First, I'd want to look at a magazine to get a picture of what we need to do."*
"I'd think of myself as a reporter and I'd conduct an interview with myself."

TEACHER: "I wonder who might help us gather resources."

At this point the teacher-librarian is asked for periodicals. Parents, relatives, and fellow teachers are canvassed for any related material.

TEACHER: "Karalee brought a National Geographic magazine that gives us some ideas. Listen to the article. What do you notice?"

The teacher listed the key ideas on the board as a beginning set of criteria for the magazine article they will soon generate. Other articles were listened to and the criteria developed. This modelling interaction activated the second half of the Writer's Cycle. (3)

The students returned to their drafts to craft their thoughts into an article. Gathered-together sources provided models to draw from as they reached to shape their thinking. (4)

After six to ten minutes, the teacher called on the group to share their beginnings. (5)

Teacher Thoughts

Once the students are comfortable with a variety of forms, they may be able to choose a form that suits their purpose.

(1) Students match purpose to form and potential audience.

(2) Students generating possibilities.

(3) The "what-struck-you" approach we learned from Donald Graves helped the students anchor content language in their mind's ear.

(4) Adult models only model the form. To refine our expression we look to student models to hear possibilities.

(5) Writers are learning strategies for transforming their raw data.

Teacher Thoughts

(6) Students are gaining skill toward becoming strategic learners.

(7) This kind of thumbnail assessment gives the teacher a reading on how the students are handling the form. It also provides student models for the class to hear.

(8) Other classes working in the same form are also an invaluable source of models.

(9) Setting purpose and recalling newly formed criteria.

(10) Sharing thinking generated by student writers. The students listen and reflect on what they hear. New perspectives are added to the developing list. Form is being built into the students' repertoire.

(11) Making the experience safe for all students.

(12) Sometimes the students like to remain anonymous (for a while).

(13) Hearing the choices strengthens everyone's connections.

(14) Students experience many possibilities before they revise their own text.

(15) One teacher printed out the revised text and gave a copy to each writing team. The teams cut up the sentences and played with their order. They presented how they would order the story and why to the whole group.

Classroom Story

The class ended with the students reflecting on what they did and why. (6)

Prior to the next class the teacher read the drafts, sorting them into five categories based on her first impressions of how well the students had captured the agreed-upon criteria. (7)

She drew samples to read to the students. (8)

With the first drafts completed, the next class began with:
TEACHER: "We were working to turn our thinking into a magazine article. What did we think made a good article?" (9)

The teacher listed the criteria on the blackboard in column 3. The blackboard is set up like this:

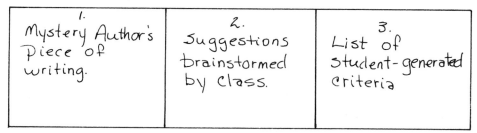

1. Mystery Author's Piece of writing.	2. Suggestions brainstormed by class.	3. List of student-generated criteria

TEACHER: "Let's listen to two or three of the drafts we wrote yesterday to see if we might add anything new to our list. The writers will remain anonymous until they choose to identify themselves. (10)

"Doing a group edit will help us to see what works well. I have asked a mystery writer permission to work with her piece of writing. (11) You will all get turns being the mystery writer. You won't have to identify yourself unless you want to. This is one way we can help each other learn new skills." (12)

The teacher either has the text on the chalkboard or she has printed it on chart paper.

The students heard the piece of text. They looked at it in light of the first criterion listed on the board. For the article the students had chosen "exciting beginning" as the first criterion. Suggestions for improvement were listed on the board in the middle column. (13) The group heard all of the possibilities, then voted to establish the best choice. The text was changed and then it was examined with the second criterion in mind - clear writing that creates an action picture.

The piece of writing was processed four times, each time from a different perspective. (14) The suggestions were listed, the students voted, and the text was altered. Sometimes little change was needed.

Many teachers reflect that this group process provides the modelling and skill-building necessary for the students to revise alone. (15) The teaching team at South Carvolth School have taken the process one step further.

Classroom Story

They place the students in writing teams, mixing able with not-yet-able students. Teams of two or three seem to work best. When students meet in their writing teams, they use the same criteria the whole group used to process individual pieces. (16) Bob McNeil at Simonds School arms each writer with an editing sheet. They record suggestions offered by their team. Later they reflect on the suggestions as they revise.

Proofreading can follow the same group, team, and individual process as editing. In this stage students apply what they know and prepare for a conference.

TEACHER: "Many of you are finished your drafts. What will you do next?"

STUDENTS: *"I will read it out loud to see if it makes sense. Then I'll find an editor."*
"I'm going to cut mine up and reorganize the thoughts."
"I'm ready to do my personal audit. First I'll take my ruler and read line by line, circling words I think are spelled incorrectly. I'll check my dictionary for words I may have. Then I'll check my Can-Do List to see what I have to do." (17)

TEACHER: "You really are a writer.

"When you are ready for a conference, put your name on the blackboard. I'll come to you. If you are waiting, take out your sketch book and work on the illustrations for your piece. (18)

"Who is ready to see me now? Great. I'll be right there, Kelly. Get your writing folder. Have your Can-Do List ready. You could put on today's date. (19)

After the conference Kelly moved over to the computer for word-processing. A parent aide was ready to process her text. As early as Grade 2 in some of the classes, students are drafting onto the keyboard. The computer, for them, is just a special pencil.

Our parents play a vital role by helping with word processing, locating books for illustrating, assisting at the publication stage, and providing audiences for eager young writers. We call them "Parents: Partners in Publishing."

Near the end of the Writers' Workshop time, groans can be heard when the teacher announces:
"Boys and girls, our time for working on our pieces of writing is almost over. Look back on what you've accomplished today. In ten minutes be ready to come to the group and share. You may want to bring something to show us or you may just want to tell us where you are in the process." (20)

Teacher Thoughts

(16) Writing is drafted in one sequence but text can easily be moved around, especially if classes have access to computers or scissors.

(17) A Can-Do List is generated by the teacher. It focuses on what the student can do in the form(s) being mastered. Our Can-Do Lists are in the student writing folders along with their personal drafts being published.

(18) Donald Carrick encouraged us to have students sketch from pictures, models, and books, and then to bring these illustrations through drafts before publication.

(19) In the conference, the student and teacher dialogue around ideas, word choices, and sentence length and variety. Mechanics are looked at once the thinking has been refined. One teacher moves around the room carrying a stool. The stops to "chat" are short, yet they help to move the young writer forward.

(20) Students are in different stages. By hearing how other young writers work, they confirm the "okayness" of playing with possibilities that leads each writer to his or her own unique expression. Powerful thought is recognized immediately.

One teacher graphs the students in the different stages of this phase of the cycle.

Sharing accomplishments builds satisfaction.

Extensions

1. Presenting assemblies feature writing. Tyson School plans a Young Authors' Conference every two months. The students prepare pieces of writing for the event. The day begins with a visiting author sharing his or her writing experiences with eager young listeners. Families, friends, and community members gather in the afternoon to hear each student share writing in Kindergarten to Grade 7 groups. Behind the podium stands an ever-more-confident young writer. His or her expression of personal best is genuinely received. Individual expression is received in total quiet. Thought is celebrated.

2. You may find it useful to use the graph adapted and expanded by Jane Hunter:

Different Forms That Writing May Take

Purpose	Writing Form
To Record Feelings, Observations, etc.	●personal letters ●science reports ●poems ●jottings of sensory impressions from an experience - physical education, music, drama, story, art, etc. ●diaries, journals
To Describe	●character portraits ●reports of a sequence of events ●labels and captions ●advertisements
To Inform or Advise	●posters (advertisements) ●scripts for news broadcasts ●minutes of meetings ●invitations ●programs
To Persuade	●advertisements and commercials ●letters to the editor ●notes for a debate ●cartoon captions
To Clarify Thinking	●note-taking for research topics ●learning logs ●explanations of graphs and diagrams
To Explore and Maintain Relationships With Others	●letters ●making requests ●greeting cards ●questionnaires
To Predict or Hypothesize	●speculations about probable outcomes in health, science, social studies topics ●endings for stories

To Make Comparisons	● charts ● note-making ● diagrams, graphs ● descriptions
To Command or Direct	● recipes ● instructions ● stage directions ● rules for games, safety
To Amuse or Entertain	● jokes, riddles, puzzles ● scripts for drama, puppet plays ● stories and poems ● personal anecdotes

From R. D. Walshe, *Every Child Can Write.*
Adapted and expanded by Richmond School
District Elementary Vice Principal, Jane Hunter.
Printed with Permission.

3. Beyond Presenting

What we do with the published work is an important part of the process.
The parents at Aldergrove School made cloth-covered files 28 centimetres
wide and 46 centimetres long to house publications. Velcro fasteners rip
open as students prepare to choose and share their writing. The students
are gaining a sense of authorship so we look for ways to focus on their
polished thinking.

— Prepare displays featuring authors. Each author can show all of the
resource material used to help with the text.
— Have the students choose powerful lines from their texts and create a
book or a wall display.
—Take the polished work and turn it into another form. Last year one
teacher had her students turn one draft into a great sentence, a letter, a
descriptive paragraph, and two kinds of poetry.
—Save three pieces each year to mount in a blank book that moves on
with the student. What a treasure to take with you from school!
—Have the students choose a piece of published writing to put in a
school anthology or newspaper. Some schools find strong community
support by publishing school collections of student writing.

Talking to Teachers

We wanted to close with the voice of classroom teachers—field researchers of our learning strategies. Opportunities gleaned in working side-by-side with these professionals have truly helped polish our thinking.

Colleen Politano, a K-2 teacher, workshop presenter, author, and winner of the Hilroy Award, the Canadian Teachers' Federation's National Award for Innovative Projects, reflects on the collaborative nature of her classrooms.

> Sharing literature and letting children in on the secrets of print, modelling writing, and solving problems together reward me with days filled with purpose and joy.

Judy Alden, a Grade 1 teacher, writes to us of the changes she sees in her classroom.

> I now use strategies I have learned from studying the reading/writing process. We do clusters across the curriculum in reading, spelling, phonics, mathematics, science, social studies, art, and so on. I am less tied to guide books and I take the time required by the class to master a particular style or topic. The process is the focus; the product is not the most important element.

She shares two writing samples from the same class and reinforces the pride of student authors, regardless of skill level.

My Grade 1 student proudly reads her writing to me:

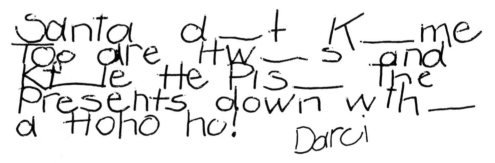

"Santa just came to our house and carefully he placed the presents down with a Ho Ho Ho!"

Another writes:

> *A piece of ice cracked. Father was scared and terrified. Mother was too. The egg slipped. Father was too terrified to speak. A killer whale came. The penguins were terrified and scared. Then a seal came.*
> Adam

Gerry Gilker, Grade 1/2 teacher and former school administrative assistant, notices how

> time passes quickly for students and teachers because of high interest and on-task engagement.

Gerry celebrates the passing of the three reading groups.

Rose-Amy Akune, Grade 2 teacher and teacher-librarian Grades 1 to 10, echoes Gerry's thinking.

> The strategies that extend children's thinking and allow them to have self-esteem reinforce my belief that I'm on track.

In our travels from school to school, we have noticed this calm confidence of teachers as they challenge the learning opportunities for their children.

Cheryl Macdonald, Grade 2/3 teacher and editor of *Prime Areas*, the British Columbia Primary Teachers' Journal, believes the extensive prewriting has made a significant difference.

> This year, I have made one basic change and have noticed another qualitative leap in my students' writing. I have found that when given extensive prewriting experiences, they write with much more personal knowledge, feeling, confidence and commitment, and use more precise and sophisticated vocabulary.

Here is a sample of writing from a student in Cheryl's most recent class.

I'm am a fat insect. Its not a thrill but thats life. When I was flying I saw something shiny. I went to see what it was. It was a spider web and I flew right in to it. The spider felt the vibrations. I was terrified. The big spider climbed up from its nest and wrapped me in soft silk. Two days later the spider came again and her fangs sunk deeply in me.

Jennifer
Year 3
Sept. 30, 1987

The power of writing as a learning/thinking tool permeates classrooms at all levels and across all curriculums. Susan Kovach, a senior secondary teacher, writes,

> I never thought that writing could be a part of the science curricula. It amazes me how creative students can be and how, through writing, they can understand the science concepts much better. In addition, I assumed that if you gave students higher level questions it would make them think. It never occured to me that one should teach students the tactics or strategies that would enable them to think.

Principal William McLeod reinforces Susan's words.

> These strategies provide children with confidence that they can indeed do what they came to school to do - read and write. They love to write! You might ask: Everyone? My answer is: It is very hard to find an exception.

Donna Nanson and Maureen Van De Walle, Consulting Teachers with an elementary Diagnostic Centre, have shared in this "every child can participate and succeed" experience.

> We discovered ways to use the strategies to enhance learning for students with specific learning problems. We introduced strategies in the Diagnostic Teaching Centre using story grammar, imagery, and clustering.

Such changes echo through our classes. Pat Tipple, Grade 5/6 teacher, explains,

> Today I find that as much as 80 per cent of the story's discussion has been done and we've perhaps only just begun to read. We predict, we anticipate, we image, we make decisions before we read. The greatest thing is that there are no discipline problems and no one sees himself as a poor reader in the low group.

This power of collaborative thinking for all, in mixed ability classes, moves into secondary situations as well. Des McKay, Social Studies Department Head and Grade 9/10 teacher/counsellor, writes,

> I have found that by using the reading/writing process strategies, I can effectively challenge each student in my class at his/her level. This allows the weaker students a voice and a share in the class. I am convinced that the higher test scores I am getting are the direct result of having the students become active learners rather than passive sponges who absorb information but seldom use it in a way meaningful to them.

Grade 7 teacher and Computer Helping Teacher K-12 Aileen Lew explains that word processing adds a further dimension.

> Students, once introduced to word processing, are soon drafting on the computer, revising and editing and proofreading as a natural progression to the publication stage.

We honour these changes. Wayne Hamilton, secondary English teacher, reflects on the experience of participating in a strategy.

> We tried to get these images into word clusters before they would escape us.

This engagement in task is evident for all learners.

In conversation, Principal Alan Warburton, Vice Principal Linda Kaser, and Kindergarten teacher Gayle Mosher summarized the changes they had experienced.

> Teaching is way more fun! You are celebrating each child's thoughts as a learner. Part of the fun is knowing what this is doing for them. We believe we are preparing learners, especially if we begin in primary and we follow all the way through.

The joy of learning together is echoed by Intermediate Helping Teacher Sheila Borman.

> To watch a colleague take a risk, to hear a group of teachers use a shared language in discussing learning theory, to know how they value the experience of working and thinking together about their teaching practices, makes this year one of the most rewarding in my career.

We celebrate not just student results, but teacher recognition of the effort, the effect, and the result.

As child-centred professionals, we are developing the eyes, the ears, and the voices of reflective practitioners. Together we are working to develop students who are competent with language and with people.

Pamela Wood, Grade 3/4 teacher, synthesizes the changes she sees.

> The greatest gift to the teacher in all this is the changed attitude to writing among the children. They enjoy writing, they choose to write sometimes in their spare time; they have lots of ideas that they are willing and able to express; they show respect to others who write; they notice writing techniques in the things they read or which are read to them.

Our goal for students is an increasing ability to become introspectively critical of their power as learners. From the many student writing samples we have read, we chose to end with a sample from Grade 7 teacher Cindy Culbert. Bernice, a student who had previously been failing social studies, explains what she now knows about learning.

> *Final Message*
>
> *This report had a lot of things done to it: revisions, drafts, and brainstorming. The reason why I think it will get a good mark is because I was a picture on the wall watching them do the steps of mummification. I would sit alone in a quiet room and think of all the things I knew of being mummified. Then I would write notes on what I saw and turn them into sentences.*
> Bernice

Bibliography of Research Materials

Alvermann, Donna E. 1987. Integrating oral and written language. *Research Within Reading: Secondary School Reading,* ed. Donna Alvermann, David W. Moore, and Mark W. Conley. Newark, Delaware: International Reading Association.

Alvermann, Donna E., Deborah R. Dillon, and David G. O'Brien. 1987. *Using Discussion to Promote Reading Comprehension.* Newark, Delaware: International Reading Association.

Attwell, Nancie. 1987. *In the Middle.* Portsmouth, N.H.: Heinemann.

_____. 1985, March. How we learned to write. *Learning:* 51-53.

Avery, Carol S. 1987, October. First grade thinkers becoming literate. *Language Arts,* 64: 611-618.

Bagley, Michael T. 1987. Imagery to Develop Memory. New York: Trillium Press.

_____. 1987. Using Imagery in Creative Problem Solving. New York: Trillium Press.

Bagley, Michael T., and Karen Hess. 1984. *200 Ways of Using Imagery in the Classroom.* New York: Trillium Press.

Barell, John. 1985, April. Pre-Conference Institute, Association for Supervision and Curriculum Development Convention, San Francisco, CA.

Bean, Wendy, and Chrystine Bouffler. 1987. *SPELL by Writing.* Rozelle, New South Wales: Primary English Teachers Association.

Belliston, Larry, and Marge Belliston. 1982. *How to Raise a More Creative Child.* Allen, Texas: Argus Communications.

Booth, David. 1987, October. Presentation at the British Columbia School Trustees Association Conference, Vancouver, B.C.

Brandt, Ronald S. 1986, May. On creativity and thinking skills: a conversation with David Perkins. *Educational Leadership:* 12-18.

Brown, Ann L. 1985, April. *Teaching Students to Think as They Read: Implications for Curriculum Reform.* Urbana-Champaign: National Institute of Education Reading, Education Report No. 58.

Brown, Barbara. 1980. *Supermind.* New York: Harper and Row Publishers.

Brown, Jason W. 1980. Brain structure and language production: a dynamic view. *Biological Studies of Mental Processes,* ed. D. Caplan. Cambridge, Mass.: M.I.T. Press: 287-300

Bruner, Jerome S. 1986. *Actual Minds. Possible Worlds.* Cambridge, Mass.: Harvard University Press.

Buchanan, Ethel, ed. 1984. *For the Love of Reading.* Winnipeg, Manitoba: C.E.L. Group.

Buckley, Marilyn Hanf. 1986, April. When teachers decide to integrate the language arts. *Language Arts,* 63:369-377.

Buzan, Tony. 1982. *Use Your Head.* London: B.B.C. Publications.

Calkins, Lucy McCormick. 1986. *The Art of Teaching Writing.* Portsmouth, N.H.: Heinemann.

_____. 1983. *Lessons From A Child.* Exeter, N.H.: Heinemann.

Carbo, Marie. 1987, October. Matching reading styles: correcting ineffective instruction. *Educational Leadership:* 55-62.

Carrick, Donald. 1983, July. Presentation at the Bellingham Reading Conference.

Changeux, Jean-Pierre. 1985. *Neuronal Man.* New York: Oxford University Press.

Close, Susan. 1986. Deepen comprehension and expand written expression. Richmond, B.C.: *Teacher as Researcher.*

Close, Susan, and Linda Wingren. 1986, Winter. Freeing the children to write. *Prime Areas.* British Columbia Teachers' Federation.

Cochrane, Orin, Donna Cochrane, Sharen Scalena, and Ethel Buchanan. 1984. *Reading, Writing and Caring.* Winnipeg, Manitoba: Whole Language Consultants.

Collins, Allan, John Seely Brown, and Susan E. Newman. 1987. *Cognitive Apprenticeship: Teaching the Craft of Reading, Writing and Mathematics.* Champaign, Illinois: University of Illinois Centre for The Study of Reading, Technical Report No. 403.

Combs, Martha. 1987, January. Modeling the reading process with enlarged texts. *The Reading Teacher,* 40,4: 422-426.

Costa, Arthur L. 1985. Developing Minds. Alexandria, Virginia: Association for Supervision and Curriculum Development.

Costa, Arthur L., and Robert J. Marzano. 1987, October. Teaching the language of thinking. *Educational Leadership:* 29-33.

Di Pardo, Anne, and Sarah Warshauer Freedman. 1987, May. *Historical Overview: Groups in the Writing Classrooms.* University of California, Berkeley: Centre for the Study of Writing, Technical Report No. 4.

Donaldson, Margaret. 1978. *Children's Minds.* Glasgow, Scotland: William Collins Sons.

Duffy, Gerald G., and Laura R. Roechler. 1987, January. Teaching reading skills as strategies. *The Reading Teacher,* 40, 4: 414-418.

Fehring, Heather. 1987, March. Cooperative learning strategies applied in the language classroom. *Read Around Series,* ed. F. Gollasch, Australian Reading Association, No. 1.

Fisher, David. 1987, Spring. What are we talking about? new book guides writing teachers. *Research Forum:* 4-7

Flood, James, ed. 1984. Promoting Reading Comprehension. Newark, Delaware: International Reading Association.

Fox, Mem. 1987, January. The teacher disguised as writer in hot pursuit of literacy. *Language Arts:* 18-32.

_____. 1987. *Teaching Drama to Young Children.* Portsmouth, N.H.: Heinemann.

Fulwiler, Toby. 1986. Journals across the disciplines. *To Compose: Teaching Writing in the High School,* ed. Thomas Newkirk. Portsmouth, N.H.: Heinemann.

Gambell, Trevor J. 1986. Literature: why we teach it. *English Quarterly.* Wininpeg, Manitoba: CTE, 19:83-91

Gentry, J. Richard. 1987. *Spel... Is a Four-Letter Word.* Richmond Hill, Ontario: Scholastic.

Goodlad, John I. 1984. *A Place Called School.* Toronto, Ontario: McGraw-Hill.

Goodman, Kenneth S. 1986. *What's Whole in Whole Language?* Portsmouth, N.H.: Heinemann.

Goodman, Kenneth S., E. Brooks Smith, Robert Meredith, and Yetta M. Goodman. 1987. *Language and Thinking in School.* New York: Richard C. Owen Publishers.

Gordon, Christine J. 1984. *Improving Reading Comprehension and Writing: The Story Grammar Approach.* Kimberley, B.C.: A.N.W. Learning Aids.

Graves, Donald H. 1986, May. Presentation to the Transmountain Reading Conference, Vancouver, B.C.

_____. 1983. *Writing: Teachers and Children at Work.* Portsmouth, N.H.: Heinemann.

Graves, Donald H., and Virgina Stuart. 1985. *Write From the Start.* New York: Plume.

Guthrie, John T., ed. 1981. *Comprehension and Teaching: Research Reviews.* Delaware: International Reading Assocation.

Harrison, Bernard D. 1986. The pleasure of writing. *The Writing of Writing,* ed. A. Wilkinson. Milton Keynes, England: Open University Press.

Harste, Jerome C., Virginia A. Woodward, and Carolyn Burke. 1984. *Language Stories and Literacy Lessons.* Portsmouth, N.H.: Heinemann.

Hess, Karen M. 1987. *Enhancing Writing Through Imagery.* New York: Trillium Press.

Hillocks, George Jr. 1987, May. Synthesis of research on teaching writing. *Educational Leadership:* 71-81.

_____. 1986. *Research on Written Composition.* Urbana, IL: ERIC Clearinghouse on Reading and Communication Skills, and the National Conference on Research in English.

Hirsch, E.D. 1987. *Cultural Literacy and the Schools.* Boston: Houghton Mifflin Co.

Hunkins, Francis P. 1987, November. Sharing our instructional secrets. *Educational Leadership:* 65-67.

Johnson, David W., and Roger T. Johnson. 1984. *Cooperation in the Classroom.* Minnesota: Interaction Book Co.

Johnson, Terry D. and Daphne R. Louis. 1985. *Literacy Through Literature.* Sydney, Australia: Methuen.

Jones, Beau Fly, Annemarie Sullivan Palincsar, Donna Sederburg Ogle, and Eileen Glenn Carr, Eds. 1987. *Strategic Teaching and Learning: Cognitive Instruction in the Content Area.* Elmhurst, Illinois: North Central Regional Educational Laboratory.

Joyce, Bruce and Marsha Weil. 1986. *Models of Teaching.* Englewood Cliffs, New Jersey: Prentice-Hall.

Kindergarten Curriculum Guide and Resource Book. 1984. British Columbia Schools Dept., Curriculum Development Branch.

McCleary, Linda. 1987, Winter. Shh... my students are writing: the writing process in a junior high classroom. *Canadian Journal of English Language Arts,* 10: 25-29.

McClelland, Jay L., David E. Rumelhart, and Geoffrey E. Hinton. 1986. A general framework for parallel distributed processing. *Parallel Distributed Processing, Vol. 1: Foundations,* ed. D.E. Rumelhart and J.L. McClelland. Cambridge, Mass.: M.I.T. Press.

McKim, Robert H. 1980. *Experiences in Visual Thinking.* Monterey, CA: Brooks/Cole.

Machado, Luis A. 1980. *The Right to Be Intelligent.* New York: Pergamon Press.

Marzano, Robert J., and Daisy E. Arrendondo. 1986. *Tactics for Thinking.* Aurora, CO: Mid-Continent Regional Educational Laboratory.

Michelson, Norma. 1987. Presentation to the Fraser Valley Writing Schools Network, Chilliwack, B.C.

Morris, Bert. 1987, June. Effective Reading in Content Areas. *Read Around Series,* ed. F. Gollasch. Australian Reading Association, 2: 105-108.

Moss, Anita, and Jon C. Stott. 1986. *The Family of Stories.* Toronto, Ontario: Holt, Reinhart and Winston of Canada Ltd.

Murray, Donald M. 1986. Write before writing. *To Compose,* ed. T. Newkirk. Portsmouth, New Hampshire: Heinemann.

_____. 1985. A Writer Teaches Writing. Boston: Houghton Mifflin.

Nelms, Ben R. 1987, May. Response and responsibility: reading, writing, social studies. *Elementary School Journal,* 87: 571-589.

Nessel, D. 1987, February. Reading comprehension: asking the right questions. *Phi Delta Kappan:* 442-445.

Newkirk, Thomas, and Nancie Atwell, eds. 1986. *Understanding Writing: Ways of Observing, Learning and Teaching K-8.* Portsmouth, N.H.: Heinemann.

Newman, Judith M. 1985. *Whole Language Theory in Use.* Portsmouth, N.H.: Heinemann.

Olson, Carol Booth. 1985. The thinking writing connection. *Developing Minds,* ed. A. Costa. Alexandria, VA: Association for Supervision and Curriculum Development: 102-107.

Pearson, P. David, and Robert J. Tierney. 1984. *On Becoming a Thoughtful Reader: Learning to Read Like A Writer.* Champaign, Illinois: University of Illinois Centre for the Study of Reading, Reading Education Report, No. 50.

Perkins, David. 1988, January. Art as an occasion of intelligence. *Educational Leadership,* 45: 36-43.

_____. 1981. *The Minds Best Work.* Cambridge: Harvard University Press.

Peterson, Ralph L. 1987, November. Literature points the way. *Ideas With Insights: Language Arts for Elementary School.* N.C.T.E.

Pressley, Marjorie. 1979. *The Mind's Eye.* Escondido, CA: Escondido Union School District Board of Education.

Raths, Louis E., Selma Wasserman, Arthur A. Jonas, and Arnold Rothstein. 1986. *Teaching for Thinking.* New York: Teachers College, Columbia University.

Readence, John E., Thomas W. Bean, and R. Scott Baldwin. 1981. *Content Area Reading: An Integrated Approach.* Dubuque, Iowa: Kendall/Hunt Publishing Co.

Rico, Gabriele Lusser. 1983. *Writing the Natural Way.* Los Angeles, CA: J.P. Tarcher.

Romano, Tom. 1987. *Clearing the Way.* Portsmouth, N.H.: Heinemann.

Rumelhart, David E., Geoffrey E. Hinton, and Jay L. McClelland. 1986. The appeal of parallel distributed processing. *Parallel Distributed Processing, Vol. 1: Foundations,* ed. D.E. Rumelhart and J.L. McClelland. Cambridge, Mass: M.I.T. Press.

Sanders, D.A. and J.A. Sanders. 1987. February. Capturing the magic of metaphor. *Learning:* 37-39.

Smith, Frank. 1986. *Insult to Intelligence.* New York: Arbor House.

_____. 1984. *Joining the Literacy Club.* Victoria, B.C.: Abel Press.

_____. 1983, May. Reading like a writer. *Language Arts,* 60: 558-567.

Stafford, William. 1986. A way of writing. *To Compose: Teaching Writing in the High School,* ed. Thomas Newkirk. Portsmouth, N.H.: Heinemann.

Sternberg, Robert J. 1985. *Beyond IQ: A Triarchic Theory of Human Intelligence.* New York: Cambridge University Press.

Suhor, Charles. 1988. Content and process in the English curriculum. *Content of the Curriculum, 1988 ASCD Yearbook,* Ronald S. Brandt. Alexandria, Va.: Association for Supervision and Curriculum Development.

Taba, Hilda. 1966. *Teaching Strategies and Cognitive Functions in Elementary School Children.* San Francisco: San Francisco State College, Cooperative Research Project No. 2404:39-40.

Templeton, Shane. 1986, March. Synthesis of research on the learning and teaching of spelling. *Educational Leadership,* 43: 73-78.

Tierney, Robert J., John E. Readence, and Ernest K. Dishner. 1980. *Reading Strategies and Practices: Guide for Improving Instruction.* Toronto: Allyn and Bacon.

Tovey, Duane R., Lynn G. Johnson, and Michael Szporer. 1986, October. Remedying the 180 Syndrome in reading. *Childhood Education.*

Vacca, Richard T. 1981. *Content Area Reading.* Toronto, Ontario: Little Brown and Co.

Walshe, R.D. 1984. *Every Child Can Write.* Rozelle, New South Wales: Primary English Teaching Association.

Wasserman, Selma. 1987, February. Teaching for thinking: Louis E. Raths revisited. *Phi Delta Kappan,* 68 (6): 460-466.

Weisberg, Robert W. 1986. *Creativity: Genius and Other Myths.* New York: W. H. Freeman and Co.

Wells, C.M. 1987, October. Show students how to bring writing to life. *Learning:* 40.

Wells, Gordon. 1986. *The Meaning Makers.* Portsmouth, N.H.: Heinemann.

Wilkinson, Andrew, Gillian Barnsley, Peter Hanna, and Margaret Swan. 1980. *Assessing Language Development.* Oxford: Oxford University Press.

Wilkinson, Andrew, ed. 1986. *The Writing of Writing.* Milton Keynes, England: Open University Press.

Williams, Linda Verlee. 1983. *Teaching for the Two-Sided Mind.* New Jersey: Prentice-Hall.

Wilson, Paul T., Richard C. Anderson, and Linda G. Fielding. 1986, January. *Children's Book Reading Habits: A New Criterion for Literacy.* University of Illinois at Urbana-Champaign: Center for the Study of Reading, Reading Education Report No. 63.

Bibliography of Stories and Poems Used in Classroom Scenarios

Brinckloe, Julie. 1985. *Fireflies.* New York: Macmillan Publishing Co.

Cave, H.B. 1978. Two Were Left. *SRA Reading Laboratory 2C.* Willowdale, Ontario: Science Research Associates, Inc.

Cebulash, Mel. The Flowers. *Action Unit Book 3.* U.S.A.: Scholastic Book Services, Inc.

Cochrane, Orin. 1986. *The Great Gray Owl.* Winnipeg, Manitoba: Whole Language Consultants.

Fox, Mem. 1987, January. Swans and Peacocks. The teacher disguised as writer in the hot pursuit of literacy. *Language Arts:* 18-32.

Rawls, Wilson. 1974. *Where the Red Fern Grows.* New York: Bantam Pathfinder.

Wilder, Laura Ingalls. 1983. Crossing the Creek. *Ripple Effects.* Toronto: Nelson Canada.